An outline of
SOCIOLOGY
as applied to Medicine

An outline of
SOCIOLOGY
as applied to Medicine

David Armstrong MB BS MSc LRCP MRCS
Unit of Sociology as applied to Medicine
Guy's Hospital Medical School
London

Bristol
John Wright and Sons Ltd   1980

Published by John Wright & Sons Ltd., 42–44 Triangle West, Bristol BS8 1EX.

British Library Cataloguing in Publication Data
Armstrong, David
    An outline of sociology as applied to medicine.
    1. Social medicine
    I. Title
    301.5   RA418

ISBN 0 7236 0565 3

Printed in Great Britain by
John Wright & Sons Ltd., at The Stonebridge Press, Bristol BS4 5NU.

To
MY PARENTS

Preface

This book has emerged in response to an increasing concern with behavioural science in the curricula of many health professionals. Students in these areas, I believe, need a concise textbook that will enable them to grasp the relevance of sociology to medicine. This book attempts to meet that need and I hope that it will be of interest to undergraduate and postgraduate students of medicine and the related health disciplines.

The 'biological' framework of the traditional health sciences is for the most part self-evident and students are expected to study the particular details of these subjects. However, in sociology students will find that much of the framework is new and that coming to terms with it can be a difficult task. Moreover, unlike the biological sciences, the results of detailed sociological studies are more likely to vary with changes in social values, behaviour, attitudes, organization, etc. This book therefore tries to meet these points by offering an outline or 'map' of sociology's relevance to medicine. Comprehensive details of particular sociological studies and tables of sociological data have been avoided in the belief that these can be more usefully obtained from journals, course work or later, during clinical practice.

Areas of sociology—particularly theoretical—which do not have any direct application to medicine are for the most part omitted. I have tried to avoid specific sections on sociological concepts or methods in isolation from medical issues; instead important sociological ideas are presented in the context of medical practice. Thus the emphasis is on clinical relevance and clinical relatedness.

Specific references have been left out of the text on the grounds that most would be redundant for the anticipated readership and the fact that the book does not attempt to be a comprehensive text in medical sociology. However, a short list of further reading, which interested students might like to pursue, is provided at the end of each chapter.

David Armstrong

Acknowledgements

This book has evolved over several years teaching a course to medical students at Guy's Hospital Medical School. Their response to the course has influenced my ideas on the teaching of the subject and has therefore had an important effect in shaping the form and content of this book. Two students, Steve Wood and Phillip Razzell, were kind enough to read and comment on earlier drafts and I am particularly grateful for this 'consumer' opinion. John Weinman, a colleague at Guy's, has argued through various ideas with me. My secretary, Bessie Higgins, has typed various drafts with consistent good humour. Finally, I have to thank my wife, Pauline, for her encouragement and helpful comments on the final draft.

Contents

1 *Introduction: Health as a social concept*

Approaching sociology for the first time students versed in the natural sciences often experience difficulties. Compared with anatomical structures or physiological processes society can seem very abstract and sociologists themselves at times seem divided as how best to investigate social phenomena. Much of the contribution of sociology to medicine, however, should present few problems and that part which breaks new ground can be grasped once the principles underlying it are seen.

Three broad themes are covered in this book.

1. *Social factors in health and illness*

The processes of becoming and being ill can be divided into various sequential stages.

    a. Aetiology of the problem.
    b. The problem.
    c. The decision to visit the doctor.
    d. The doctor–patient consultation.
    e. The response to treatment.

At each of these stages we can try to answer the question: What factors in the social environment influence becoming and being ill? The answers to this question should complement the explanations based on biological factors with which many students are more familiar.

2. *The social construction of medical reality*

Perhaps more difficult to grasp is the notion that our basic concepts about the world—including those of medicine—are socially derived. This notion in part stems from a widely held belief that our knowledge or concepts directly correspond with the reality of the 'world out there'. This belief in its turn depends on believing that the acquisition of knowledge about the world is a passive process: we simply look at phenomena and allow the resulting observations to flow freely into our minds.

But seeing, experiencing or knowing the world is not a passive process. If the average layman is asked to describe a chair he will describe a structure with a seat, four legs and a back. A scientist interested in ergonomics or in mechanical engineering might describe a totally different perception. The structure described depends on preconceived ideas built up from knowledge and life experience in a particular social context.

A middle-class child of a stable marriage might describe marriage in terms of a union between one man and one woman characterized by human exchanges which reflect consideration, compassion and endearment. The child of a broken marriage in the slums of Glasgow might describe the same phenomenon in terms of drunkenness, argument and physical violence. In both these examples the individual concerned perceives the physical structure or personal relationship in terms that reflect his own personal experiences in the social setting in which he is brought up. When he looks at chairs or at marriages he has already defined both subjects in the light of his experience and relates what he sees to his preconceived ideas.

This point is of crucial importance for it means that what we see or know of the world is in part a product of how we organize or classify it. Furthermore, how we organize our sense data is not immutably fixed by some biological parameters, as we can observe other societies with other patterns or see differences within our own cultures over a period of time. It seems that in various ways—from parents, from schools, from our social environment—we learn how to see the world. Our knowledge, attitudes and beliefs, though they might seem to be very personal and individual, in fact derive from society. In this way our reality is 'socially constructed' and this construction forms the basis of one aspect of sociological study.

Thus our notions of health, disease, symptoms, normal functioning, illness, etc., are socially derived and an important part of the sociology of medicine is to investigate how they arose, how they are maintained and their implications for health and the health services.

3. *Providing health care*

Finally this book covers aspects of the provision of health care. In part this draws on work in economics and social administration, but it is presented in the context of the meaning of health.

In summary, though this book is divided into individual chapters and contains, running throughout, these three approaches to medicine, the underlying theme is the problem of health. Whether it is in understanding why people go to the doctor, what is meant by the term disease, or investigating the advantages of different means of providing health care the question, What is health?, remains of paramount importance. In broad terms the answer can be given: health is a social concept. The following chapters attempt to illustrate and clarify this statement.

Reality is "socially constructed".

thus our notions of health, disease, symptoms, normal functioning, illness etc. are socially derived + play

2 *Going to the doctor*

It might seem reasonable to suppose that people consult their doctor when they experience symptoms. Yet there are two aspects of people's behaviour which seem incongruent with this view of the symptom as a trigger to seek help.

i. There are people who fail to go to the doctor, or go very late, despite experiencing symptoms of serious disease. This group constitutes what has been termed the 'clinical iceberg', in that it seems that there are more people who have serious symptomatic disease not under medical care than there are receiving treatment.

ii. There are people who attend the doctor with trivial or relatively minor complaints. Many general practitioners believe that between a third and a half of their patients fall into this category.

What then is the relationship between the experience of a symptom and the decision to consult a doctor?

2.1. Symptom prevalence in the community

Symptoms seem to be experienced very frequently. One survey found that when shown a checklist, adults could recall on average about four symptoms in the previous two weeks. Another found that over 95% of people experienced at least one symptom in the previous two weeks, and researchers who persuade people to keep a daily health diary of symptoms they experience find that noting down a symptom every day is not uncommon. Many of the variations in results found in these surveys reflect differences in the ability to remember symptoms. Thus, if asked to recall how many symptoms they have experienced in the last two weeks, people seem to remember about two. If on the other hand they are invited to note down the symptoms they have experienced at the end of every day in a 'health diary', symptoms are recorded much more frequently. Moreover if respondents are asked to keep

4

health diaries for themselves and for their families, the number of symptoms recorded is invariably greater in their own reports than for those of their spouse and children. This may be due to a failure of other members of the family to report all their symptoms, to a failure of the respondent to record them or to the involvement of the respondent in the research leading to increased awareness of their own bodily processes. It has been found, for example, that a proportion of respondents keeping health diaries over several months drop out of the survey after a few weeks claiming that the constant recall of symptoms is making them feel ill.

While these various responses to the experience and recording of symptoms pose particular problems when it comes to measuring symptoms in the community and interpreting the findings, it is still possible to derive several general conclusions from the surveys that have been carried out.

   i. Symptoms are very common. Most people experience symptoms regularly in their daily lives.

   ii. It seems that most reported symptoms are felt to be inconsequential. Most symptoms seem transient and are soon forgotten.

   iii. It is not so much the actual symptom—a pain, a small haemorrhage—which influences patient response but the meaning placed on it.

   iv. Both the actual perception of the symptom and the meaning placed on it can vary according to its context, the patient's mood, etc.

   v. A symptom may be thought of as trivial by the doctor and serious by the patient and vice versa.

Why then do people visit their doctor or seek other help for their symptoms?

2.2. Illness behaviour

Given the wide prevalence of symptoms in the community it is clear that only a small selection of these are brought to the doctor. Whereas people probably experience symptoms several times a week, they go to see their doctor on average only 3 or 4 times a year. The reason for this difference cannot be explained solely by reference to the severity of the symptoms as some people experience serious symptoms and delay consulting the doctor whilst others seem to attend readily with minor complaints.

To answer the question of why patients go to the doctor sociologists have offered the concept of 'illness behaviour' which describes how individual patients, through a series of decisions, negotiate a 'career' from being a well-person to being an ill-patient. This process has various stages which are set out below. Clearly not every stage may be important in bringing the patient to the doctor, but it can be useful to consider the process as a series of potential questions posed by every patient.

"Concept of Moral Career"

1. *Are my symptoms normal or abnormal?*

a. Certain symptoms are classified as normal because of their wide prevalence in society. Headaches for example are so common that only about one in 200 is presented to the doctor; those that turn up tend to be unusual in some way, perhaps in frequency or context. Anthropological studies confirm that there are certain widely experienced symptoms which are socially acceptable because of their ubiquity. It has been reported that in one South American tribe a certain facially disfiguring skin disease is so common that it is the tribe members who don't have the disease who are labelled abnormal and seek 'treatment' from the local medicine man.

b. Normality may not only be defined by reference to the total society but also to smaller groupings within the community. Every member of a society belongs to a number of such sub-groups and will therefore tend to accept the norms of these groups with regard to symptoms and illness. For example, one of the expectations of old age is that more general aches and pains will be experienced than in younger people. The experience of such symptoms may be seen as normal by many old people and many may be tolerated without bothering the doctor.

Even when the patient presents to the doctor, this 'normalization' may block the emergence of important diagnostic information. Thus it is common while taking a medical history from a patient who smokes to find that he denies having a cough. On prompting he often remonstrates, 'Oh, its only a smoker's cough.' The patient has interpreted 'Do you have a cough?' as 'Do you have an abnormal cough?' to which, for a patient who coughs every morning and perhaps lives in a household of similar people, the answer is no.

c. Earlier events may also be called upon to normalize the presence of a symptom. For example, a rodent ulcer might be seen as a bruise which has not healed from an earlier bump on the forehead or the lump of a breast cancer might be explained away by some half-forgotten injury; as it grows very slowly in size its characteristics are not seen as abnormal as it increasingly 'has always been like that'. It is sometimes only when the cancer breaks down and fungates that the patient comes to the doctor complaining of the abnormal and socially unacceptable smell.

2. *Should I go to the doctor on this occasion?*

The significance of symptoms to the patient seems to lie in whether they are perceived as 'normal' or 'abnormal'. It seems therefore it is not symptoms *per se* which take people to the doctor but the assessment of them. It is possible to break this assessment down into five 'social triggers' which together encompass the various ways in which symptoms come to be seen as abnormal. They are:

a. Perceived interference with vocational or physical activity. As vocational or physical activity is a part of 'normal' life then symptoms which interfere with it must be abnormal. Allowances must be made however for the type of work or activity: a cut finger may interfere more with a typist than a car driver and some physical disability may only become apparent to a sedentary office worker if he plays a game of football one day.

b. Perceived interference with social or personal relations. Similarly, symptoms which interfere with normal social interaction will be more likely to cause concern. Consideration must be given to the patient's usual pattern of interaction which may differ for different occupations, ages, etc.

c. The occurrence of an interpersonal crisis. This upsets the everyday equilibrium people seem to have with many of their symptoms. Some change in personal relationships can change the perception of an otherwise innocuous symptom or seemingly decrease the tolerance to chronic pain or disability. The patient with long-standing osteoarthrosis who presents with joint pain after 'coping' for a long period may in fact be triggered by a domestic crisis rather than by an exacerbation of the underlying condition.

d. A kind of temporalizing of symptomatology. Though the symptom may or may not interfere with work or social relations it may still be seen as unusual or ambiguous. If this is the case then some deadline is set for the symptom. This may be a time deadline such as, 'If this symptom has not disappeared by Monday then I shall go to the doctor', or it may be a frequency deadline such as, 'If I have more than two nose bleeds this week . . . .'

e. Sanctioning. This refers to pressure from friends or relatives to visit the doctor. It is not uncommon for a patient to open the consultation with, 'I did not want to bother you doctor but . . . insisted I should come.'

3. *What else could I do?*

There are four alternative courses of action.

a. Ignore the symptoms.

b. The patient may consult with friends and relatives. It has been suggested that the advice given by friends and relatives constitutes a lay referral system, analogous to the medical referral system, in which the patient is referred to lay consultants with successively greater claim to knowledge or experience of the symptom in question. It has also been suggested that the lay referral system for a tight-knit community may act as an alternative health care system. As most symptoms are probably self-limiting this alternative system may in effect limit the demand for medical services.

c. The patient may self-medicate. It has been reported that in a 2-week period people take, on average, about two different medicines each. About two-thirds of these are not prescribed by the doctor but are bought directly from the pharmacist. About 10 different types of medicines can be found in the average home at any one time so it would seem people have good access to 'self-medication'.

d. The patient may consult the medical services, most commonly with their general practitioner.

Whether course (*d*) is pursued and the official medical services consulted can be seen as a process by which the patient compares the relative costs and benefits of such action.

4. *Will I benefit from seeing the doctor?*

The first decision concerns the perceived value of going to the doctor: will he be able to do anything for the problem?

Besides offering his sympathy and reassurance the doctor has two, more formal, functions through which he can help the patient.

a. The first is the therapeutic: the doctor can offer some form of treatment which may benefit the patient. Patients may have their own idea of what treatment the doctor can offer and this may influence the decision to consult. Some people consult their doctor expecting cures and treatments which do not exist; alternatively many people do not consult because they feel the doctor cannot do anything for them.

One study reported that among a group of patients in the year before their death many symptoms were experienced for which no medical advice was sought. 29% of these symptoms were described as 'very distressing' and 37% had been present for a year or more.

b. The second way in which the doctor can help the patient is to ease the transition from being a 'person' to being a 'patient'. Although a person may feel unwell he may not be socially accepted as being ill, for example by his employer, unless a doctor 'legitimates' his illness. In Western society only the doctor has the social authority to legitimate illness and admit the person to what is termed 'the sick role' (*see also* Chapter 5). In accepting the sick role the patient gains two benefits but is expected to fulfil two obligations. These are:

i. *The patient is temporarily excused his normal role.* Gaining a sickness absence certificate from the doctor is the obvious way in which this expectation is met. Merely visiting the doctor however confers some legitimacy on a claim to be sick. Whereas 'feeling unwell' might be treated sceptically by friends and colleagues, a visit to the doctor may be sufficient to gain credibility.

ii. *The patient is not responsible for his illness.* Not being held responsible for the illness relieves the patient of a considerable burden in our society. In some other societies the patient may be held responsible in that, for example, the illness might be believed to be a punishment for some past crime or transgression.

iii. *The patient must want to get well.* By gaining two advantages from the sick role the patient must undertake two obligations. The first is his recognition that the sick role is a temporary status which he must want to leave behind. If he apparently does not want to get well then instead of the sick role being conferred by the doctor a label of 'malingering' may be used.

iv. *The patient must co-operate with technically competent help.* The
fact that it is only the doctor who can legitimately confer the sick
role in our society ensures that 'technically competent help' tends
to be confined to the official medical services. A patient who
chooses to defer to a lay person with claims to medical knowledge,
in preference to a medical practitioner, is judged as not fulfilling
one of the basic obligations of the sick-role.

While the patient may be seeking to legitimate his illness by
visiting the doctor it does not apply to all consultations. Indeed
the value of the sick role is severely limited especially for those
with chronic illness, who are both unable and unlikely to fulfil
several of the obligations and expectations.

5. *What are the disadvantages of going to see the doctor?*

The sick role confers both obligations and expectations on the
patient. Expectations, such as being excused normal work, may
be of benefit to the patient whereas certain of the obligations such
as having to co-operate with the doctor may be counted as a
social cost. This cost is only one of many to be found in actually
using a health service. Other costs are found even when there is
no financial charge at the point of use (*see* Chapter 9), and these,
whether they are waiting lists, inconvenient surgery hours or the
time needed to go to the doctor, tend to act as disincentives to
use the service.

The other potential cost of using the health service is the
approachability of the doctor. Undoubtedly many patients are
put off going to the doctor because they believe he will not be
sympathetic to their particular complaint.

It has been found that many patients withhold complaining to
the doctor about serious symptoms because he appears too busy or
uninterested. It has also been reported that the apparent wide
variation in the numbers of patients presenting with a sexual
problem to different doctors is itself a product of the doctor's
approachability. Patients quickly establish whether their doctor
will handle a sexual problem with sympathy and understanding
or whether he will dismiss it or be embarrassed by it, and
these perceptions may well affect their decision to seek his
advice.

Importance for the doctor

The answer to the question, 'Why do people go to the doctor?' is not a simple one. What has been shown in this section is that seeking medical help is not necessarily related to the occurrence or severity of a symptom. The way in which a symptom is 'processed', both in individual and social terms, will determine what action is finally taken. Here this action has been described as a 'decision-making process' on the part of the patient. Of course not all patients follow this pattern or take all these factors into consideration. Their decision may not even seem rational to the doctor but he may not be aware of the often complex reasoning which brings a patient to the consulting room. The patient who seems off-hand, the patient who says he did not want to come but was sent, the patient who hands over a piece of notepaper with a list of his symptoms, are all to be understood in the context of a decision-making process which has often gone on several days before the patient actually reaches the doctor. To establish during the interview why the patient has come at that particular time may be of great value in both understanding and managing the presenting problem.

Perhaps the patient has unrealistic expectations of the doctor's ability and has too great or too little tolerance of different symptoms. The social trigger may give some clue as to the other reasons why a patient has consulted besides the presenting complaint. A patient may have failed to keep an appointment because the surgery was too far away, because the receptionist was too brusque or because the doctor did not offer the expected sympathy last time.

While the doctor always enquires of the particular presenting problem there is, also, always the 'second diagnosis' to be made— why did the patient come *now*? Patients very rarely come to the doctor immediately a symptom starts, most delay and wait hours, days or weeks. In many cases the actual process of becoming ill that has been described above may be more important in understanding and managing the patient's problems than the illness itself.

2.3. Illness behaviour in its social context

The above account of how people come to consult with their doctor is based on the patient as an individual who makes various individual decisions. This perspective may, as has been suggested, be useful for the doctor in establishing the particular reason the patient came and the nature of the problem with which the patient presents.

However, the above explanation of illness behaviour needs to be placed in its social context. A description of illness behaviour which deals solely with decision-making on the part of the individual patient is inadequate as a full explanation as it ignores several important aspects of the patient's social milieu. Consider the various points in the 'illness career' at which the patient's particular social context assumes importance.

a. It has been assumed that a symptom as a subjective feeling is wholly a product of the patient's personal awareness of his bodily processes. But how does the patient manage to distinguish symptoms from normal biological changes? Throughout the day various biological changes occur within the body: some, such as the digestive process, are for the most part imperceptible while others such as aches and pains, hunger, tiredness, etc., are perceived. When is tiredness abnormal? A question like this can only be answered with reference to some knowledge the patient already possesses about the limits of normal bodily functions. Such knowledge is partly derived from personal experience but this is, in its turn, shaped by socially based evaluations. Is this pain normal?—Yes, you can expect it with menstruation. Is this swelling normal?—Yes, it is a bruise caused by falling down. I feel tired—You shouldn't, you've just got up. Thus the response by people around us, by the social milieu in which we find ourselves, will over the years shape our perception of our own body and our response to perceived changes within it.

b. The 'social triggers' which are said to motivate people to visit the doctor can similarly be seen to be dependent on the patient's particular social milieu.

c. The potential choice of courses of action following the identification of a symptom is dependent on the knowledge of alternatives—and their effectiveness—that the patient possesses. Where does this come from? The lay referral system, for instance, will clearly differ for different people in different walks of life.

d. The value of going to see the doctor will depend on the relative emphasis different patients place on the benefits and costs. Yet here again patterns can be discerned. Patients with manual work who more often have to 'clock-in' compared with non-manual workers might be more likely to value a sick note or be more sensitive to the time lost in actually visiting their doctor.

Individuals in their social context

Taken together these various points illustrate one of the fundamental claims of sociology: that individual knowledge, attitudes and beliefs are derived from the social milieu in which we are born, brought up, live and work. Although people might be biologically similar, different life experiences and social relationships all go to make apparently very different people. These social backgrounds and relationships are studied by the sociologist as the 'social structure' in which the individual person exists.

Further reading

Dunnell K. and Cartwright A. 1972
Medicine Takers, Prescribers and Hoarders. London, Routledge & Kegan Paul.
   A survey of people's attitudes and behaviour regarding health and the taking of medicines.

Hannay D. 1979
The Symptom Iceberg. London, Routledge & Kegan Paul.
   A study of experience of and response to symptoms.

Tuckett D. 1976
An Introduction to Medical Sociology. London, Tavistock. *See* Chapter 5: Becoming a patient.
   A useful review of the field of illness behaviour and also a comprehensive list of references.

3 *Social structure*

Human anatomy is the study of the structure of the human body. As such it can contribute to our understanding of three questions:

i. How the whole body functions (through knowledge of its particular parts).

ii. How a single cell or group of cells functions (through knowledge of its relationship to neighbouring structures).

iii. How the human body came about (through studying its 'earlier' forms in embryology, physical anthropology, etc.).

In the same way that knowledge of anatomical structure can enable us to answer these questions, so a knowledge of social structure can enable us to answer analogous questions of the individual and society. Firstly, by knowing something of its constituent parts a society may be better understood. Thus differences between British and French societies might be identified from knowledge of their respective family networks, educational systems or legal institutions. Secondly, society—the total structure—has profound effects on individuals living in it and their beliefs, attitudes and behaviour can often be deduced from knowledge of the particular aspects of social structure within which the individuals lead their daily existence. At a simple level everyone is born into a pre-existing 'structure' and can expect to derive many of their personal characteristics from it. Someone born into a working class Catholic Scottish family is likely to have a very different life style than someone born into the English aristocracy.

The great importance of the concept of social structure lies in the fact that it is both an effect and cause of individual behaviour. People in their everyday lives create social structure yet social structure from the cradle to the grave has a profound influence on how those lives are led. As in anatomy, the reciprocal arrangement between the whole and its parts has important implications when examining either.

The final question that knowledge of social structure might help to answer is how present society or particular aspects of social structure came about. It is possible to answer partly by reference to the reciprocal relationship between individuals and social structure: society is a product of the individuals who make it up. Yet if this was the complete answer society would be static as individuals made society, and society made the same type of individuals, who then recreated the same society, and so on. It is clear that this explanation is inadequate because society does change, from year to year and from epoch to epoch. It is therefore necessary to advance other explanations of why society exists as it does today and why it changes in the way it does. As might be expected there are many such theories which the reader can find in formal sociological texts: one or two will be touched upon in this chapter. It only remains to point out that as the various theories of how the human body came about range from Genesis through competing claims on ape geneology, so sociological theories of social change are often radically different. Arguably they are also more important than theories of physical evolution in that they have direct effects on our everyday lives; less arguable is the considerable controversy to which they often give rise.

This chapter, then, examines various aspects of social structure. In the main, long lists of the attributes of these phenomena have been avoided: many of them change from year to year and current data are widely available. Instead the emphasis is on understanding the meaning of these various aspects of social structure and thereby contribute towards providing an appropriate framework for the interpretation of the relevant data on social structure and health. An example, therefore, drawn from the field of dental health is not meant to signify the profound importance of teeth for society, rather it is used to illustrate the argument being presented.

3.1. Health and social structure

In what way is a knowledge of social structure useful in an understanding of health problems? Consider an example. An important factor in dental health is the attitude of the patient to the wearing of dentures. Patients opposed to the wearing of dentures may be more inclined to care for their natural teeth than a patient who does not mind dentures. One survey asked a group of people whether the thought of wearing dentures bothered them (*Table* 1).

Table 1.   CONCERN AT WEARING DENTURES

	Bothers	Doesn't bother	Don't know
%	45	45	10

Of the population which had an opinion on the subject exactly half were not bothered with the thought of wearing dentures. However, when this population was divided into age group, sex and social class the following results were obtained. (*Table* 2.)

Table 2.   CONCERN AT WEARING DENTURES BY AGE, SEX AND SOCIAL CLASS

		% bothered
Age	21–30	40
	31–40	57
	41–50	43
Sex	male	43
	female	57
Social class	I & II	71
	III	49
	IV	53
	V	31

Instead of a group evenly divided into those concerned at the thought of wearing dentures and those unconcerned, a more interesting picture appears. Social class, for instance, seems clearly related to attitudes towards denture wearing.

This example, though somewhat trivial, nevertheless illustrates the importance of various aspects of social structure to patient *attitudes* towards dental health. These attitudes are of importance because they, in their turn, may influence *behaviour*. It has been found, for example, that frequency of cleaning of natural teeth or of visits to the dentist is also related to these aspects of social structure (*Table* 3).

Table 3.   REGULARITY OF DENTAL VISITS BY SOCIAL CLASS

	Social class				
	I & II	IIIn	IIIm	IV	V
% regular attenders	35	21	6	1	—

Finally, patient behaviour such as regularity of teeth brushing or sweet consumption may have an effect on the amount of dental disease experienced. In this case the *aetiology* of the disease may be implicated in social structure. (*See* Chapter 7.)

Thus a breakdown of data by various aspects of social structure may illustrate patient attitudes, behaviour and the aetiology of disease.

3.2. Interpreting the data

Measurement and analysis using social variables can lead to potentially interesting results; the crucial question however remains: what do the results mean? Using the data presented in *Table* 4, some common problems encountered in interpretation will be described.

Table 4. EDENTULOUS IN POPULATION BY AGE, SEX AND SOCIAL CLASS

		% *Edentulous* (i.e. with no natural teeth)
Age	25–34	7
	45–54	41
	65–74	79
Sex	male	33
	female	40
Social class	I	15
	II	31
	III	29
	IV	46
	V	47

a. *The importance of theory*

A clear gradient among those with no natural teeth can be seen running from social class I to social class V. It may simply be an artefact caused by disproportionately large numbers of old people in social classes IV and V (though one would have to explain why age was class linked). It may reflect different attitudes and behaviour towards tooth care in the social classes, both in self-care and in use of dental services. Or it may reflect differential exposure to aetiological factors or a poorer dental service for one class compared with another. Inevitably when results are open to such varied interpretation the answer to the question 'What does social class mean?' or the question 'Why do social classes exist?' will influence the choice. Those who favour the view that social class is a product of power relations in society might tend to support the explanation that it is the 'social system' that is culpable, whether by advertising and promotion of unhealthy foods or by offering inadequate dental services to some social groups. Others might favour the view that it is the inappropriate behaviour of certain social classes, whether in neglecting preventive measures or in failing to use available services, which is to blame. Which is the 'correct' interpretation can rarely be provided by the data itself, and it will be frequently found that an explanation of the wide differences between the social classes in health matters requires some recourse to a particular theoretical position.

b. Biological or social?

The other interpretative problem encountered in this form of social analysis is the conflict between biological and social explanations. Is the increase in numbers of edentulous with age caused by biological factors, social factors or a mixture of the two? Is the excess of tooth loss in women compared with men a function of biological differences or social?

The problem may be encountered when comparing attitudes of men and women. For example, more women than men report being nervous about visiting the dentist (*Table* 5).

Table 5.   NERVOUSNESS AT VISITING DENTIST BY SEX

		% *Nervous*
Sex	male	23
	female	43

These figures may reflect some innate courage of men; women may think this unlikely. The differences may, on the other hand, reflect more on the social need of men to display some bravado.

This same dilemma, of deciding whether it is biological or social factors that are of importance, is faced when explaining differences in behaviour. Women for example consult with medical services more frequently than men. Possible explanations for this are:

i. They are genuinely more 'ill' and therefore their increased consultation rates reflect their greater health need (though they outlive men by six or seven years).

ii. Women are expected to be less tolerant of minor disabilities because they are the 'weaker sex'. If this is true then the increased consultation rates of women are a product of their particular social role in contemporary society.

iii. The social role of women contributes to both a lower tolerance of symptoms and also more of them. The task of working, of bringing up children and of running a home—which many women have to face—is so stressful that it causes women to have both more symptoms and a lower tolerance threshold.

The difficulty in choosing between these respective arguments is exacerbated by the impossibility of separating symptoms from their perception and tolerance. Choosing the more likely is therefore more dependent on preconceptions about the appropriate social role of women.

The importance of stressing some of these various differences between men and women is twofold: differences in disease patterns between men and women may reflect social as well as biological differences; the attitudes and behaviour of the sexes that the doctor meets are not only due to differences in biology. A particular behaviour pattern, for example, 'menopausal symptoms', may reflect various social pressures and difficulties as well as underlying hormonal changes. In many cases it is extremely difficult to disentangle these variables but the reader should bear in mind that simply because a biological difference does exist between, say, men and women, this offers no guidance as to how much of their health or respective behaviours is biologically determined. Much of the data will equally support the view that the major determinant of sex differences in behaviour and health is social.

c. Age-related changes

Consideration of ageing as a wholly biological process, and ignoring psycho-social factors, may distort our understanding of changes occurring with old age. Firstly the actual biological impact of ageing seems to be considerably affected by various social and psychological factors. If there is a built-in biological ageing mechanism in cells, there seems to be considerable variation

in its effects between individuals and cultures. Apparent physiological changes with age probably therefore reflect both social
and biological factors in the life of the patient.

Secondly, there is the more direct influence of attitudes and
behaviour on health. It is commonly stated that 'you are as old
as you feel' and undoubtedly attitudes vary with age and have an
important bearing on the subjective state of health. Attitudes and
behaviour can also have a direct influence on aetiology and on
decisions to consult with the health services.

It has already been shown that attitudes to the wearing of
dentures varied by age. Also it is found that patient preference for
extraction versus filling for an aching tooth also varies with age
(*Table* 6).

Table 6. PREFERENCE FOR EXTRACTION VERSUS FILLING FOR AN
ACHING FRONT TOOTH

Age		% Have it extracted	% Have it filled
Age	16–34	21	79
	35+	36	64

The fact that nearly twice as many of the over 35s would prefer
an extraction compared with those under 35 may reflect one of
two quite different influences.

i. *A generation effect.* The over-35 group will have been born in
times when attitudes towards dental care may have been very
different. This attitude may then have been maintained despite
changes in the type or quality of care. The result is an out-dated
attitude towards current facilities or practices.

This generation effect becomes of greater importance in the
very old for whom current medical and dental care has changed
radically. Thus their attitudes towards the health service—such
as their frequent reluctance to be hospitalized—may reflect on
an earlier period of health care.

ii. *A cultural effect.* The other important determinant of attitudes
and behaviour of the old is the current social-cultural expectations
of society. (This notion is developed more fully in Chapter 6, on
labelling.) These expectations affect the individual directly, and
indirectly through the behaviour of others. The result is often an
approximation to the social stereotype of how that particular age
group should think and behave. A preference for extraction rather

than conservation may therefore reflect contemporary attitudes to tooth care in the elderly rather than those of an older generation.

d. Measurement and interpretation in social research

The problems of analysing data on social structure and health—some of which have been described—often present a seemingly daunting task. Moreover the sceptic can point to the added problems of measurement and data collection in the social sciences to challenge the validity and conclusions drawn from any social research. Yet these problems must be seen in perspective and their relative importance recognized. Three points can be made:

i. Social scientists are for the most part aware of these problems and have developed, and continue to develop, appropriate techniques to overcome them. Thus, for example, whereas a physiologist might try to control out extraneous variables during an experiment, the social scientist can attempt to control them statistically during the analysis, after the actual collection of data. Moreover the data itself can be collected by a wide range of different means: observation, questionnaire, interview, etc.

ii. It would be misleading to imagine that the theoretical issues and debates which often seem to characterize social research are wholly absent in biological research. Frequently the assumptions underlying biological research are not made explicit, often because there is a broad consensus on them, but this is not to imply that these assumptions do not therefore exist. Indeed it can be argued that by bringing these issues into the open (and perhaps committing hostages to fortune) the social scientist has a more rigorous approach to research than when they remain half-buried in 'time-honoured' research methods.

iii. However difficult, the ultimate purpose of pursuing research in medical areas is for the understanding it can throw on health issues. By this criterion, no matter how straightforward the research, if it does not contribute to this end then it is of no value. On the other hand if the research, though difficult, is in an area of fundamental importance to health then the results however qualified and tentative may be of great value. It is by their potential contribution to understanding health, then, that social scientists would wish to be judged. An example of one aspect of social structure which has been extensively studied—and it would seem with valuable results—is given below.

3.3. Social class

A person's occupation determines his social class (or socio-economic group). The position of a person's occupation within the wider social structure has important implications for how he spends his life: hence knowledge of a person's social class can be used to ascertain his likely attitudes and behaviour.

Is a social class, however defined, a real group in society or is it an artifical classification imposed by sociologists on a continuum of social positions? There is no simple answer. Any system of classification is artificially imposed to make a large amount of data comprehensible. The meaning of different groupings or categories is therefore given in the theory behind the classification. In biology, division into species is judged meaningful within the theory of evolution. Similarly in sociology the particular theory employed will give an answer to the question, 'What is social class?'

Social class has been extensively studied by sociologists and it occupies an important place in various theories of social order and social change. These theories range from the Marxist which identifies two main classes by their relationship to economic production: those possessing economic power and those without it. Economic power constitutes the grounds for dominance in other areas of stratification such as status, power and knowledge. Various refinements have been proposed over the years to this theory but its main thesis, that low social position is imposed on one group by another for its own ends, remains. At the other end of the spectrum lie functionalist arguments which hold that social stratification is something necessary for the 'functioning' of society. Some people must do the dirty work, some people must receive social honour, etc. Functionalism is the conventional idea put forward to explain the existence of social class—an idea, Marxists would claim advanced, by the dominant class as justification for its superior position.

The particular theory adopted will depend on (the reader's) values and these will therefore determine whether social class is seen as an evil which must be overthrown or as a necessary part of a stable society. All theories, however, acknowledge the existence of important differences between social classes and it is these which are of importance in the context of this section.

Social class was first officially used in medicine early this century when the Registrar-General classified infant mortality returns by the occupation of the child's father. These various social classes were grouped together into five main classes; these are still commonly used. They are:

Social class I: professional, higher administrative
II: administrative, managerial
III: clerical and skilled manual
IV: semi-skilled
V: unskilled

It is now usual to divide social class III into IIIn, non-manual (clerical, etc.) and IIIm, manual (skilled workers). When this is done the classification table can sometimes usefully be divided into two:

Social class I, II and IIIn:
often referred to as the *middle classes* or *white collar workers*
Social class IIIm or IV and V:
often referred to as *working class* or *blue collar workers*.

Other classifications are found 1–6, A–E, etc., but they all follow a similar pattern of distribution.

The importance of social class in the attitudes held, and behaviour shown, towards health care can be illustrated by an example (*Table* 7). In this table, taken from a survey of infant

Table 7.   CHILD REARING PRACTICES BY SOCIAL CLASS

%	Social class				
	I & II	IIIn	IIIm	IV	V
Mothers age 21 or less at first birth	24	25	40	46	53
Breast feeding at 3 months	39	34	24	22	12
Dummy at some time	39	53	71	75	74
Bedtime after 8 p.m.	7	12	20	23	26
Sleeps in room alone	54	42	20	18	3
Diet inadequate	5	10	13	13	32
Genital play checked	25	50	57	69	93
Frequent tantrums	9	8	14	15	23
High father's participation	57	61	51	55	36
General smacking	39	53	60	54	58

care in Nottingham, considerable variation can be seen between social classes; moreover, when there are significant differences, these change consistently over social class such that social classes

I and V are at opposite ends of a spectrum. Many of these patterns of infant care, whether they be length of time breast feeding, adequacy of diet or degree of father's participation, may have important influences on the future physical and mental health of the child. But equally these patterns of attitudes and behaviour on the part of the parents reveal differences between the social classes which have relevance to health on a wider scale.

Why do these differences exist? Some of them reflect the differences in *material resources* of the social classes.

The distribution of income by social class is difficult to estimate. The medium gross weekly earnings are about 25% higher for non-manual male workers than for manual workers. But these figures conceal a larger difference as they fail to take into consideration benefits from work which are not listed as earnings. In this area, which includes sick pay, company car, insurance schemes, job security, etc., non-manual workers gain significantly over manual.

The other disadvantage of an estimate of earnings at one period in time is that it ignores life-time changes. Whereas a manual worker is earning far more than, say, a medical student at age 21, their life time earnings are very different. The non-manual worker tends to be on highest salary in late middle age while a manual worker will be on peak earnings in perhaps his early thirties and thereafter witness a progressive decline or stagnation until retirement.

The difference in financial resources of the social classes is also reflected in their housing. Almost 90% of Social Class I own their homes as against 20% of Social Class V who do so. The quality of housing in the latter group is, as might be expected, worse in terms of rooms per person and in amenities such as having a bath or shower. (More recent government publications can be consulted for details of these differences.)

It must be remembered that these facts and figures about social classes are probabilities: all working class people are not necessarily worse off than middle class people in the same way that all appendicitis does not present with pain in the right iliac fossa. The actual presence of pain however means that the clinician must consider appendicitis in the differential diagnosis. In the same way the patient's social class, derived from his occupation, should alert the doctor to the possibilities of life style that this might indicate.

Yet the variation between, as well as among, the social classes in their financial and material resources is not the only significant variable for the doctor to be aware of. Consider two items from the variations in patterns of infant care (*Table* 7). A relatively inadequate diet in the working class and a late bed-time may reflect material deprivation, perhaps not enough money to buy proper food and not enough bedrooms for the child to sleep in other than the parents' living room. But equally these two habits may owe more to 'culture', that is to beliefs and attitudes, than to money. An inadequate diet may reflect the purchase of inappropriate and nutritionally poor food, and the late bed-time may reflect particular working class behaviour rather than poverty of accommodation.

Thus despite there being financial and economic reasons for some of the practices listed in *Table* 7, some can also be explained in terms of a different *pattern of culture* which produces different attitudes and behaviour, in breast feeding, smacking or father's participation in child rearing, etc.

This is not necessarily to minimize or ignore the material differences between the social classes. The relationship between structure, which determines occupational position and therefore financial rewards, and culture is a complex one and both, it may be argued, are mutually reinforcing (though it seems that at least in the short-term particular patterns of culture continue even when financial rewards are improved).

The doctor for his part needs to be aware of both cultural and material aspects of social class. When recommending a change of job, a holiday, regular bathing, etc., these need to be evaluated in the light of how realistic they are, given the opportunities and resources available to the patient. Class attitudes are also important. Most doctors, drawn from middle class families, will be fully aware of the nuances of middle class attitudes and behaviour. Middle class behaviour is characteristically described as showing 'deferred gratification', that is the person will think ahead and prepare for the future. Thus middle class people will believe in the benefits of education, of insurance, of paying off a mortgage, etc., while the working class will tend towards gaining immediate benefits from any resources they possess.

The relevance of this difference is clear when preventive medicine is considered, for working class people seem much less likely to seek out and use it. They are, for example, less likely to have their children immunized and more likely to smoke. This difference, to reiterate, may not be based on 'ignorance' or 'fecklessness' but on a different way of seeing life and a concomitant different style of living.

Failure to use services, however, is not wholly a consumer problem: equally important is how they are provided. A seven point scale has been suggested to describe just some of the possible differences in presentation of any health service (*Table* 8).

Table 8. WAYS OF PRESENTING HEALTH SERVICES

---

1. *Provision:* it exists but we challenge you to find out.
2. *Offer:* we will tell you of its existence.
3. *Invitation:* we would like you to avail yourself.
4. *Encouragement:* we will go to some trouble to convince you of the benefit.
5. *Persuasion:* we will make you feel guilty if you decline.
6. *Pressure:* we will reward you if you do, or exert sanctions if you do not.
7. *Compulsion:* we have passed a law.

The under-use of preventive services by working class people may then reflect more how those services are provided than of attitudes to health. (*See* Chapter 9 for further discussion.)

3.4. Medical intervention and social structure

Enough has been described to illustrate the importance of social structure to medicine. Knowledge of attitudes and behaviour derived from social structure may be important for the doctor, enabling him better to understand and treat his patient's problems. In particular this applies to his understanding of the patient's response to symptoms, his behaviour during the consultation and his compliance with medical advice. Furthermore the implications of aspects of social structure, particularly social class and the family, in the aetiology of disease is also important (*see* Chapter 7). In these respects, knowledge of social factors in illness can complement knowledge of biological factors in patient management.

However, though social and biological factors might function as complementary influences on the course of illnesses and their management, they are not wholly equivalent. The doctor always remains outside the patient's biological identity as an observer but he is both observer and participant in the patient's social reality. In other words, the doctor and other health workers occupy a position, as professions, in the social structure and they too have particular attitudes and behaviour towards health which might well have important bearings on the patient's problem.

Because of their specialized knowledge and skills the health professional has a special claim to be in a position to know more about health than lay people. Thus, for example, in assessing dental health the dentist might justifiably have claim to know better than the patient (*Table* 9). The boxed figures in *Table* 9

Table 9. PATIENT AND DENTIST ASSESSMENTS OF DENTAL HEALTH

| | | Patient | | |
		Good	Fair	Poor
Dentist	Good	87	10	3
	Fair	70	25	5
	Poor	53	33	14

indicate where there is agreement; where there is a difference between dentist and patient, as when over half of patients the dentist claims have poor dental health believe theirs is good, then there might seem reasonable grounds for accepting the dentist's verdict.

But consider another area where there is difference of opinion between dentist and patient, in this case over the 'fit' of dentures (*Table* 10). Again the agreements have been boxed. It will be

Table 10. PATIENT AND DENTIST ASSESSMENTS OF DENTURE FIT

| | | Wearer | |
		Good fit	Bad fit
Dentist	Good fit	48	3
	Bad fit	40	9

noticed that there are 40% of wearers who believe they have a good fit despite the dentist's view to the contrary. Who is right here?

The answer is not so clear because an assessment of 'fit' must inevitably involve some patient views. It is clearly unsatisfactory if the dentist says dentures fit perfectly when the patient is in considerable discomfort. On the other hand the dentures may be a 'bad fit' from the dentist's point of view because they could, to his knowledge, be improved. In this example there is no clear priority to be given to either patient's or dentist's views: the correct assessment probably lies somewhere in between.

Now most health problems involve the patient's views: in experiencing symptoms, in deciding to consult the doctor, in evaluating therapy, in being satisfied with the result, etc. It is clearly unsatisfactory for the doctor to say 'You are completely healthy', when the patient feels very ill. So, in the evaluation of health it seems reasonable for the doctor to be careful to ensure that patient views are heard and respected. This means that the different attitudes and behaviour produced by aspects of social structure are not to be discarded as wrong, inappropriate or stupid; instead they must be taken into account when diagnosis and treatment is taking place. When the doctor is considering a problem of health, that health belongs ultimately to the patient and the patient's perceptions must therefore be counted in management and in evaluation of the effectiveness of therapy.

This concern with the patient as a person rather than a repository of some obscure pathology might seem self-evident and desirable. However one aspect of the doctor's task is inevitably to intervene in people's lives and respect for the patient as a person is often compromised. For example, what happens when, in middle class or medical terms, some aspect of working class behaviour damages or potentially damages health? To what extent is the doctor justified in trying to alter some culturally determined pattern of behaviour, with which the patient is content, in the name of health? Respect for the patient is not merely a passive slogan but is a belief which is constantly fought-for, compromised, negotiated, over-ruled, but hopefully never forgotten.

Further reading

Worsley P. 1970
Introducing Sociology. London, Penguin. *See* Parts 2 and 3.
  A good discussion of social structure.

Social Trends. London, HMSO.

An annual compendium of government social statistics which includes a chapter on health.

The General Household Survey. London, HMSO.

Results of an annual government survey into people's attitudes, circumstances, behaviour, etc.

Includes a chapter on health.

Leeson J. and Gray J. 1978
Women and Medicine. London, Tavistock.

An analysis of women as patients and providers in the NHS.

4 *The social basis of disease*

In the last two chapters the contribution that sociology can make to traditional medical practice has been described. The next few chapters explore the relationship between medicine and society-at-large. These chapters offer a different approach to phenomena for which readers may feel they already have an understanding. Whereas a common emphasis in medicine is on disease as a biological process and on the doctor as skilled in understanding and managing that process, the following chapters examine both the nature of disease and the role of the doctor as social phenomena.

The justification for examining medical practice in this way is twofold:

a. An understanding is relevant to medicine because it helps to clarify the logic underlying some useful sociological concepts (*see*, for example, the discussion of labelling in Chapter 6).

b. It offers a basis on which many of the criticisms of medicine can be understood and possibly challenged (*see*, for example, Chapter 5).

4.1. Defining disease

The first step in an exploration of the social role of medicine is to analyse the nature of disease.

In any discussion of what constitutes good health the concept of disease has an important part to play. Yet whereas definitions of health involve judgements on the part of both doctor and patient, knowledge of the nature and characteristics of disease is peculiar to the medical profession. Patients claim to be ill, doctors decide whether they have a disease or not. Yet although doctors rarely have any problem in describing the characteristics of specific diseases there does seem some difficulty in defining what 'disease' actually is.

One approach is to break the term 'disease' down into its constituent parts, *dis-ease*, which suggests one meaning for the concept. Dis-ease, however, places the basis of disease firmly with the patient and becomes synonymous with the lay concept of illness. This is unsatisfactory as it ignores three factors.

a. The claim of the medical profession to an exclusive skill in identifying disease quite independently of whether the patient feels ill or not.

b. The 'objective' status usually afforded disease as against the more subjective experience of the patient.

c. The existence of pre-symptomatic diseases which do not immediately cause dis-ease.

Another approach which incorporates these factors, is to view disease as a 'real' biological phenomenon; this is the traditional medical view. The problem with this approach is twofold: though the characteristics of specific diseases have been identified, as has been pointed out there is no such agreement on what disease, as a group noun, actually is. Secondly great numbers of 'conditions' for which there is no known biological basis, e.g. most psychiatric diseases, are not encompassed within the definition.

Although most diseases undoubtedly do have a biological basis this is not sufficient to explain the nature of disease itself. An alternative approach to the problem is to start from the idea of what is normal.

4.2. Normality in medicine

The medical concept of disease closely embodies notions of abnormality (or pathology) as opposed to normality which denotes the absence of disease. A cancer is viewed as pathological or abnormal, as is a myocardial infarction, and so on. In this way pathology and normality seem to be two sides of the same coin and it may therefore be instructive to examine the nature of medical normality as a means of establishing what is pathology, and hence disease.

There are two ways of interpreting the term 'normal'.

'normal' - widely accepted"

a. Statistical

In this sense normal is the 'usual'. It may be given by the average or it may be described by some measure of central tendency.

There are, however, two problems in using the statistical meaning of normality as a basis for disease.

i. Statistics can provide no hard and fast boundary between normal and abnormal. They can tell which measurement is more or less normal but not the point at which it becomes 'abnormal'. This problem may not arise in conditions in which the difference between normal and abnormal is clearly distinct but many physiological and biochemical parameters are continuously distributed and the exact cut-off point where normal variation becomes pathology is difficult to establish, e.g. diabetes, hypertension, etc.

ii. There are so-called 'pathological phenomena' or 'processes' which are statistically normal in some populations. In Western countries, for example, it is actually abnormal to have atheroma-free arteries though such a condition is viewed as healthier than the presence of atheroma.

iii. There are many 'abnormal' or 'unusual' biological states and processes in which it would seem absurd to suggest that the patient is diseased. An unusual eye colour, tallness, high I.Q., long hair, etc., might all be abnormal but still construed as 'normal variations' rather than diseases. Thus statistical techniques cannot of themselves determine which biological parameters are to be considered as potential bases of disease.

b. Social or ideal

This is the second way of defining normality. In this sense the normal is that which prevalent social values hold to be acceptable or desirable. The advantages of using this social definition of normality to explain the nature of disease are several.

i. The socially acceptable or desirable is very often equivalent to the statistically common. Thus the concept embraces many of those diseases that exist apparently because of their unusualness. Moreover, because the socially acceptable may vary for different communities this definition will accommodate variation in the ascription of disease across social groups. Thus the slowing in psychomotor performance with old age, though a decline from the pattern of youth, is still normal in view of social expectations.

ii. If normality is defined by reference to the socially acceptable then disease becomes a phenomenon which leads to (or may lead to) undesirable social consequence. (The notion of 'responsibility' tends to separate it off from other states which lead to similar consequences. *See* Section 5.2.) This fixes the boundary between normality and abnormality among continuously distributed variables. A blood pressure or a blood sugar level is pathological when it may lead to potentially undesirable consequences for the patient. Difficulty in drawing that boundary reflects the unknown implications of an apparently small rise in blood pressure or blood sugar.

Moreover psychiatric disease, which could not be accounted for by exclusively biological notions of disease, is not a problem if a social definition is used. The patient who claims to have two identities contravenes our basis assumption that people only have one: this break with (our) rationality means the patient is diseased. Or the patient who campaigns against the government in a state in which political dissent and criticism is irrational (in that it contravenes the dominant culture) is similarly held to be psychiatrically ill. The question is not whether such people are 'really' diseased or not but whether the social criteria by which the disease is established are justified.

iii. It clarifies the debate about whether or not certain 'abnormalities' are to be classified as diseases. Is sickle-cell trait a disease? Only in so far as it confers no advantage on the patient or his progeny in a non-malarial country. Is homosexuality a disease? It depends on whether the condition is viewed socially as an abnormality or as a normal variation. Conflicts over its disease status merely reflects the lack of consensus in society over its social acceptability. Does dyslexia ('word blindness') exist as a disease in a pre-literate society? No, because it confers no social disadvantage.

Use of social criteria to define disease also explains the frequently experienced difficulty of distinguishing between involution and pathology in old age. It is well established that with age various physiological or involutionary changes occur, in particular degeneration of various tissues. Degeneration of tissues, however, is also a characteristic of pathology. In short, disease and involution manifest themselves in similar changes: so how are they to be distinguished?

While biologically these two phenomena are inseparable, they can be separately defined socially by reference to expectations of old age. Roughly, if the change is expected then it is involution, if it is unexpected it is pathology. Of course our expectations can vary over time and place but in general, our current perceptions of what old age *should* be like—perhaps mobility and a full life or perhaps slowing and withdrawal—will define the limits of the pathology of the aged as against what is to be construed as 'natural' bodily changes.

In summary then, the conclusion to be drawn from the above argument is that disease, while it may or may not be constituted in biological terms is always based on social values.

4.3. The biological basis of disease

Where does this leave modern scientific medicine? If the diseases which it treats are ultimately socially defined how can this be reconciled with the known biological basis of many diseases?

The answer is that though socially defined, once such categories are established it is possible to look for associated biological phenomena. Thus pneumonia may be a disease because it leads to socially undesirable discomfort, loss of normal social function or even death, but its identification depends on raised temperature, distinctive chest sounds, leucocytosis, etc. In effect, diagnosis becomes a process of 'pattern recognition' of the biological correlates of disease. Moreover, the biological character of the disease enables treatment to be appropriately directed.

An analogous situation might be that of the architect, who looks at buildings through his social eye—what is it used for, what are its aesthetics, etc.—but who requires knowledge of the physical properties of the materials used to construct it. The bricks and mortar only make a building when they are put together with a social purpose. The important point is not that buildings—and by analogy diseases—are exclusively either social or physical/biological phenomena, rather they can be described in either way. Sometimes the biological basis of the disease may be of paramount importance especially when biological/pharmacological treatments are available, but equally it can be useful to view disease as a social phenomenon for the light it can throw on the role of medicine in society.

Further reading

King L. S. 1954
What is disease? *Philosophy of Science* **21,** 193–203.

One of the earliest papers to point out that disease is based on social values.

Freidson E. 1970
Profession of Medicine. New York, Dodd, Mead.
    See Chapter 10 for a further discussion of this topic.

e.g 3.

Homosexuality + any other sexual deviance 'was' considered 'pathological' although no biological deviance. This was due to the socially accepted view of normal / abnormal.

Now, h.s. not considered path. Purely due to changing social outlook.

(It is often useful to view disease as a social phenomenon? — it throws light on the role of medicine in society.

5 *The social role of medicine*

This chapter examines the doctor–patient relationship in the light of the preceding discussion of the social values underlying the medical definition of disease.

5.1. Illness as deviance

There are usually two parties to the consultation: the patient and the doctor. The patient's role in the consultation is to present symptoms to the doctor which, in the context of the patient's life, are recognized as deviant, i.e. unusual or inexplicable. Thus: The patient presents personal deviance.

The doctor's role on the other hand is to assess the problem with which the patient presents and to give advice. Traditionally this assessment is effected by taking a history, making an examination and possibly arriving at a diagnosis. But the diagnosis of disease (or the absence of disease) is also, as has been argued in the previous chapter, a means of identifying phenomena which are judged socially abnormal or undesirable. In effect, the doctor is evaluating the patient's problem against criteria of social deviance. Thus: The doctor evaluates problems by socially acceptable criteria.

Putting statements (1) and (2) together a reciprocity in the doctor–patient relationship can be seen. In diagnosis the doctor is juxtaposing what *is* considered socially deviant against what the patient imagines *might* be socially deviant. The patient's underlying question when presenting with a symptom, whether it seems organic or psychological, is: Am I normal doctor? or, Is this abnormal doctor? to which the doctor replies in terms of current social values.

Some examples may help illustrate the argument.

a. A patient breaks a leg. There will be an accord between doctor and patient with many problems that are presented because they

36

are both aware of the implications of the presenting problems. A broken leg will therefore be recognized, as much by the doctor as by the patient, as a condition requiring treatment.

b. A patient feels tired and wants to be excused work. The doctor examines the patient, finds nothing wrong and declines to give a sick-note.

Here the doctor represents the widely held social view that people should work. Not working is a state only to be countenanced if the patient's symptoms might signify some disease which poses a greater threat to social values.

c. A patient complains of acne. The doctor gives a prescription.

In this case the doctor concurs with the patient's belief that this skin lesion is socially undesirable and therefore gives appropriate treatment.

d. A patient complains of insomnia for two nights. The doctor declines to give sleeping tablets.

Here the doctor evaluates what is socially acceptable in sleeplessness and concludes that two nights is not long enough to constitute a serious problem. Perhaps if the patient reported two weeks of insomnia it would be treated differently. Undoubtedly these limits would be drawn differently by different doctors but this medical ambivalence only reproduces the general uncertainty about how much sleep loss people should be expected to tolerate.

e. A patient presents with shortness of breath. The doctor diagnoses chronic bronchitis.

Shortness of breath is not of itself significant: it is a normal experience after a period of fast running. What the patient is reporting is that this time it seems to occur at inappropriate times. The doctor's task is to judge whether the patient's perception is correct and that the shortness of breath really does interfere to an inappropriate degree with everyday life. If the doctor thinks it does, then he can relate the symptom to 'impaired' lung function and a particular 'pathological process'. On the other hand, similar shortness of breath and the same impairment of lung function in a 90-year-old may not be judged pathological simply because it is not held to be inappropriate for such a patient.

f. A patient requests that a doctor withholds treatment for a terminal illness. These situations present dilemmas for the doctor because there is conflict of social values. On the one hand the general view in our society is that death is an undesirable outcome. (Again it is worth noting that death is a social event as well as a biological one. In certain situations in various communities—the old in a nomadic tribe, the martyr, the political prisoner who starves himself—death may be seen as a desirable end because it serves to reinforce the integrity or social goals of that community.) In Western society, however, strenuous attempts will be made to maintain life, though even these may vary from country to country. In the United States for example doctors may stress the maintenance of life, at whatever cost, more than their colleagues in the United Kingdom.

On the other hand, freedom from pain and suffering and the patient's right as an individual to have some say in his future are, like the undesirability of death, widely held social values. Thus when the patient wants to die it falls on the doctor to resolve the conflict. In some situations drugs can relieve the pain and the patient's right to a part in the decision can be reduced if it is believed that because of the imminence of death he is not 'rational' (because the desire to die offends fundamental social values it is easy to label it as 'irrational'). The dilemma arises for the doctor when he is certain that the patient 'really does want to die'.

The reader may at this point feel the argument has strayed a long way from the doctor–patient interaction as he understands it—or even has experienced. This does not mean, however, that the reader's perceptions are 'wrong', only that a different perspective on the same phenomenon can illustrate some of the wider implications of medical practice. In the above discussion this approach has hopefully thrown light on some ethical problems in medicine, and its implications for the role of medicine are discussed below.

Dr. supports socially-accepted 'norms' and treats his patients accordingly.

5.2. The doctor as agent of social control

In its role of arbiter of social values medicine acts as an institution of social control and the doctor as an agent of social control. By constantly reaffirming the boundaries of social normality the doctor serves as a support for the maintenance of social order.

This social control function is not unique to medicine: it has been, and still is, carried out by other occupational groups such as the Church and the Law.

a. The Church

Especially in earlier times the Church was the ultimate judge in matters of social values and behaviour. The Church legislated on acceptable social conduct and at the interpersonal level accepted the penitent's confession of offences against these rules. The confession was an admission of personal deviance which received affirmation and absolution from the priest who drew from his wider knowledge of what was and what was not admissible thought and behaviour.

b. The Law

With the decline of religion in modern times the rules governing social conduct have increasingly been taken over by the Law. Men are believed to have full responsibility for their actions and when they transgress the law they must be judged and punished. As with the Church, the Law both constitutes a body of knowledge (the rules) and a procedure by which those who have broken those rules have their innocence or guilt judged and acted upon. Though the defendant's plea in a court of law forms a part of the assessment of the case the ultimate judgement of innocence or guilt is independent of the defendant's belief about the rightness of his own actions. The judgement is, in effect, a juxtaposition of the defendant's personal behaviour (established by the court) and socially accepted rules of conduct embodied in the law.

c. Medicine

It is fairly obvious that the law is an institution of social control but perhaps less so for medicine, partly because deviance in medicine is usually couched in terms of abnormal biology rather than behaviour, which tends to conceal its social basis. Even so, as has been argued earlier, underlying these biological phenomena are fundamental social values.

Thus like law, medicine is a body of knowledge embodying social values (disease) and incorporates a procedure by which patients are judged ill or well by the doctor. As in law too, this judgement occurs independently of the patient's own beliefs. These beliefs may be of value in reaching a diagnosis but it is often the case that the patient is judged to be ill even though he believes himself to be well, e.g. in pre-symptomatic screening tests, or is judged well even though he sees himself as ill. Thus in the same way that the law upholds norms of social conduct, medicine too can be seen to be upholding social values and to a certain extent social conduct (though the latter is gaining more emphasis —*see below*).

To argue that medicine is engaged in 'social control' is not to say that doctors are some sort of secret policemen. All it means is that medicine, like many other apparently innocuous social activities, such as bringing up children, reading a textbook, going to school, watching television, etc., controls aspects of knowledge and ideas which support the existing social order or system.

Once this is established many other aspects of the sociology of medicine tend to fall into place. The 'sick-role', for example, which was described in Chapter 2 as a benefit which can be conferred on the patient by the doctor, can now be seen in context. The four expectations and obligations really only make sense if viewed in their relationship to medicine's social role.

The sick role

1. *The patient is temporarily excused normal social roles.* The power to legitimate sickness absence is vested in the medical profession and provides an essential element in social control in that commitment to work is a central value of our society.

2. *The patient is not held responsible for his illness.* The ascription of responsibility is an important factor in differentiating a medical from a legal problem. Law holds the miscreant responsible for his actions whereas medicine does not. For example, whether the murderer is to be viewed as a criminal to be punished by prison or a patient to be treated in a psychiatric hospital depends on whether or not he was responsible for his actions. Similarly if a shoplifter can establish that due to some hormonal imbalance, e.g. during the menopause, she was not responsible for her theft, she becomes a medical rather than a legal problem.

In many ways it is somewhat arbitrary whether people are held responsible for their actions or not. Ultimately it is underpinned by a philosophical debate over freewill and determinism rather than a dispute which can be settled with recourse to 'evidence'. Because of this the boundary between medicine and law is often blurred and it is open to medicine to 'invade' areas of human conduct traditionally maintained by legal mechanisms. Indeed it has been claimed that medicine is increasingly intruding into new areas of human conduct and using its powerful social position to legislate on appropriate and inappropriate behaviour. This process of 'medicalization', as it is called, is discussed in Chapter 8.

A further aspect of non-responsibility concerns preventive medicine. Seemingly one of the benefits that medicine can confer on the patient is freedom from feeling responsible for the illness. Unlike many other agencies of the welfare state there is apparently no need for the patient to feel guilt or failure at having to consult a doctor. This undoubtedly helps explain why many 'problems of living' are brought to the doctor rather than to other professionals (such as social workers, marriage guidance counsellors, housing officers, etc.) because the latter may be seen to hold the patient, at least in part, responsible for their actions or current situation.

However, as mentioned above the denial of responsibility is always somewhat arbitrary and it is quite possible to 'blame' patients for having disease. Cigarette smokers who present with lung cancer or ischaemic heart disease could be held to be partly responsible for their predicament if they knew beforehand of the dangers of smoking yet still continued to smoke. In this situation, however, it would seem foolish to apportion blame because it is too late and little can be gained by it.

On the other hand, if patients are held responsible for their health this may encourage them to take preventive measures. It is increasingly suggested that the days in which governments could improve the nation's health without the active involvement of the people, e.g. in sanitation, in providing clean water, etc., are now passed. Prevention, it is argued, now rests with individuals who must change unhealthy behaviour patterns if they are to avoid ill-health. (The emphasis on personal responsibility for health is also, of course, a political issue as it makes important assumptions about the control people can exert over their own lives in contemporary society.) There is thus a stress on personal responsibility in the language of disease prevention. A by-product of the success of this approach, however, might be to place a stigma on many diseases. The result paradoxically could well be a decreasing inclination to consult the doctor for these 'preventable' diseases because of the blame and guilt attached to them.

This problem can be seen in those medical problems which already have a measure of responsibility attached to them. These range from attempted suicides who, in as much as they are directly responsible for their condition, often seem to receive less sympathy from medical staff (though if they are 'really' ill with, say, severe depression then attitudes might change) to the guilt surrounding venereal diseases for which, through extra-marital sexual intercourse, the patient is held responsible. In the latter the feelings of guilt are catered for by anonymity during treatment while publicly strenuous attempts are made to 'de-stigmatize' the disease, so help will be sought early.

3. *The patient must want to get well.*

4. *The patient must co-operate with the doctor.* Both of these obligations serve to uphold the legitimacy of the social control functions of medicine while at the same time ensuring that they are effective. Just as the defendant must recognize the authority of the court (otherwise he is in contempt) so the patient must defer to the authority of the doctor. Failure to do so involves removal of the benefits of the sick role such that the patient is not considered ill so much as a 'malingerer'.

Thus it can be seen that medicine operates as an important agency of social control in our society through its authority to confer the sick role and through the very act of diagnosis. The other area of medical practice which is important in this context is 'labelling'.

Further reading

Zola I. K. 1972
Medicine as an institution of social control. *Sociological Review* **20**, 487–504.

Johnson T. J. 1972
Professions and Power. London, Macmillan.
Examines the power, status and organization of the medical profession in terms of its control over determining the patient's health need.

6 *Labelling behaviour*

The concept of deviance is a social one. The height of someone taken from the tail of a normal population distribution is 'abnormal' to the extent that it, say, lies outside two standard deviations of the mean, but it is only 'deviant' if it is in some way held to be socially abnormal. Startlingly blue eyes may be remarked upon as unusual but the person is unlikely to be cast as deviant, unlike perhaps the albino whose eye colour is both unusual and socially strange. Deviance therefore implies some degree of negative social evaluation.

But why is it that of two unusual eye colours one is deviant and the other is not? Why is it that a man who talks to himself in church is praying while a man who talks to himself in the street may be mad? 'Labelling theory', as it is often called, has been developed to help answer these questions. It is divided between two notions of deviance, primary and secondary.

6.1. Primary deviance

The concept of primary deviance relates to the actual defining of a state or behaviour as 'deviant'. Thus the act of diagnosis, of affixing disease labels to people, is a process of classification by which people are labelled ill (deviant) or healthy.

Labelling as a means of creating diseases must be distinguished from the cause of diseases. The cause of someone being ill or healthy is to be found in the preceding events which had as their consequence the particular state of illness or health. But whether they are ill or healthy, as argued in Chapter 4, can only be discerned by reference to social values. Disease or physiological state might therefore be caused by a biological organism but at a separate level it is created by the doctor when he makes the diagnosis.

The labelling of primary deviance is important because it enables apparently similar phenomena to be separated into what is socially acceptable and unacceptable. A gang of working class teenagers who break windows in a public building might be labelled as 'vandals', but would a group of drunken medical students after a rugby game be similarly charged? To many people this latter behaviour—though it is the same as the former—would be considered 'high spirits' rather than vandalism. Similarly if a person claims with some conviction that he is Napoleon it might be considered good acting if he is on the stage or schizophrenia if he is in the doctor's surgery. Again the behaviour in both instances may be virtually the same but the social interpretation, and therefore the label, differs.

The labelling of primary deviance is therefore a means by which the normal is reaffirmed and the deviant identified. Labelling in this sense serves to delineate the boundaries of what is considered to be normal social values and behaviour. From this perspective diagnosis is a process of labelling of primary deviance which defines the bounds of social normality, especially in that disease categories themselves embody such evaluations. (*See* Chapter 4.)

6.2. Secondary deviance

Secondary deviance refers to the change in behaviour that occurs as a consequence of labelling. Strong social pressures tend to promote behaviour in conformity with the label and labelling thereby becomes a 'self-fulfilling prophecy'.

The pressures on patients to change their behaviour arise from the social meaning and significance of the label the doctor has applied. A blind person may be seen as quiet and docile, a psychiatric patient as mad, an epileptic as violent. These particular stereotypes may affect both the patient's perception of himself and the responses of friends and relatives to him.

The interpersonal behaviour of a labelled person may be affected as people respond differently towards him. This response, whether it is based on an attempt to ignore the patient or help him, can reaffirm the new self-image of the labelled person. Do people talk to the blind person on the bus in the same way that they talk with other people? Some people can become quite embarrassed when they suddenly discover that the person they were talking to at the table is paraplegic: what had they been saying? Had they inadvertently said things which may have shocked or hurt?

The response of so-called normal people to disability or stigma of some form may be well-meaning but the result can often be to bring the behaviour of the person so labelled into conformity with people's expectations. There is some evidence, for example, of a 'halo' effect in the classroom such that if a teacher is told that certain children are intelligent, even if they are only of medium ability, the labelled children achieve better results then seemingly similar ability children.

The other means by which behaviour towards stigmatized people, particularly the mentally ill, differs, is that it often goes back into their past life to find events and behaviour which will make today's label seem a reasonable judgement. This process of 'retrospective interpretation' occurs in everyday interaction and is also commonly found in the media. The suicide of an apparently contented public figure seems perplexing until past events, perhaps a bout of depression five years ago, make sense of the event. But does it? Most of the people who have bouts of depression during the past five years do not commit suicide. And what of the last four years of contentment? Why does a depressive episode of a few months' duration several years ago matter more than the recent mood? The answer is that the present is comprehended and interpreted by reference to the past, if necessary distorting the past to make it justify the present.

In many ways a doctor's notes are distortions of past events because they are selective. They don't record when the patient does not have headaches or was very happy, only when the headaches occurred or when the depressive bouts erupted. This is not to argue that the current basis of writing case notes is wrong, only to point out that one of the unintended consequences of this practice may be to reinforce in the doctor's mind the correctness of the current diagnosis.

6.3. Relevance of secondary deviance to medicine

The notion of secondary deviance is of importance to medicine in that certain disease labels carry with them public stereotypes which may change a patient's behaviour. Thus a man fully recovered from a myocardial infarction may refuse to return to work and become a near invalid who is confined to the house because of the image he and his family and friends have of the 'coronary cripple'. A diagnosed epileptic may refuse to climb stairs, go swimming or cross a busy road, he may become depressed and withdrawn, again because of the social meaning placed on his diagnostic label.

In many cases these consequences are almost unavoidable, it is only by giving the patient a diagnosis, whether it is blindness, epilepsy, S.T.D., etc., that adequate treatment and care can be arranged for the patient. In other cases the effect can be lessened if the doctor is aware of the potential stigma the diagnosis carries and therefore handles it more cautiously. In other words a diagnosis is not simply a convenient classification given to some underlying biological phenomenon; it may also be a label which carries significant social meaning. To tell a patient he has Hashimoto's disease will probably draw a blank, but to tell a patient he is a diabetic or an epileptic may well set in motion significant changes in his life as a direct consequence of the social meaning carried by the diagnosis. In the end these changes may have a greater effect on the patient's life than the biological dysfunction which was originally described.

6.4. Institutionalization

A particular variant of secondary deviance of importance to medicine is the process known as 'institutionalization'. It is now well established that if a person is placed in an institution such as a prison or a mental hospital for many years then their attitudes and behaviour change. It is clear that in an institution with its own sets of rules and routines, inmate behaviour, however resistant at first, will gradually change towards conformity, if only to make the daily routine more manageable.

This process of conformity is often considerably aided by the practices of many institutions which have the effect of 'depersonalizing' the inmate on first admission. Personal effects are rarely allowed and private space or activities are kept to a minimum. The effect is to reinforce the exclusion of the inmate's 'old' self and the emergence of a new institutionalized identity. Inmates must adjust to new routines of sleeping, eating, relaxing, defaecating, etc., which have often been introduced for the benefit of the staff and institution than for the needs of the patient. (*See* Section 9.4, on Goal displacement.)

The problem with this new identity and adjustment is that though it might be suitable for living within an institution it is inappropriate for life outside. In particular the dependency which institutions create in their inmates means that they have great difficulty in adapting to independence outside its walls. Dependency is of course exacerbated by the fact that most of those hospitalized for a long period are precisely those who through mental or physical impairment are unable to cope.

These effects are well known and there is now a policy to try to prevent institutionalization by keeping people in the community for long-term treatment. Otherwise some of the effects of institutions can be minimized by shortening the length of each stay and by trying to reduce some of the more stark depersonalizing features of an institutional atmosphere. Moreover, even when treatment does require lengthy hospitalization specific attention can be directed towards maintaining or re-establishing the patient's autonomy through some form of mental or physical 'rehabilitation'.

6.5. Labelling and psychiatric disease

Secondary deviance has been extensively used to analyse psychiatry. This is probably for three reasons:

i. Psychiatric diagnosis is less precise than diagnosis in the rest of medicine with the result that it is easier for the critic to dispute the existence, type or natural history of psychiatric disorder.

ii. Unlike most organic diagnoses, psychiatric conditions carry much greater social significance. Madness for centuries has been the basis of many and various social theories and practices.

iii. The manifestations of mental illness are principally in changed behaviour, and as labelling too may lead to altered behaviour, it may be difficult to distinguish the relative effects of the mental illness itself from the effects of the labelling.

The importance given to labelling in psychiatry does vary from psychiatrist to psychiatrist. Most would now acknowledge its value in explaining some psychiatric problems; some go so far as to suggest that it can explain all psychiatric morbidity. Three types of argument can be identified.

a. Psychiatric illness is a consequence of the labelling of primary deviance. The main proponent of this view is Thomas Szasz who argues that mental diseases do not exist in the same way as organic diseases. Psychiatric diseases are only metaphors: some people have 'sick' minds in the same way as some economies are 'sick'. The people currently labelled as mentally ill are those whose slightly incongruous behaviour has been labelled and therefore treated by psychiatrists. Psychiatrists don't identify 'real' disease, they label 'inappropriate' behaviour which is not in any way 'diseased'.

Szasz's argument seems to founder on his assumptions with regard to organic disease in that he believes the latter to be somehow 'real'. But organic disease only differs from psychiatric disorder in the existence of biological correlates; both however identify anatomical, physiological or behaviour changes which it is believed are socially disadvantageous. (*See* Chapter 4.)

Thus when Szasz claims that psychiatric disease only 'exists' because it is labelled that way he is not offering a special insight, for this can be argued in all disease. Moreover such an argument does little to help people who suffer from 'psychiatric phenomena', whatever their status, and it fails to appreciate the way in which social phenomena can have 'real' effects on people's lives.

b. Psychiatric illness is a consequence of the labelling of primary deviance and the resulting secondary deviance. This view holds that psychiatrists identify a behaviour pattern which though it may be slightly unusual is still within the normal range, label it as psychiatric disease (i.e. primary deviance) and by a process of investigation and treatment induce the mental illness that was first labelled (i.e. by secondary deviance). The power of this argument stems from two factors:

i. The supposed unsettling impact for someone who is told they are or might be mentally ill (patients are still often referred to the 'nerve doctor' because of the negative social evaluation placed on many aspects of psychiatric illness).

ii. The investigation and treatment environment places the patient in an abnormal situation in which the 'correct' behaviour is difficult to establish. On the one hand 'normal' behaviour is clearly abnormal in a mental hospital, and on the other hand abnormal behaviour merely fulfills the psychiatrist's predictions.

An illustration of this was an experiment conducted in a State hospital in the USA. The researcher and his co-workers all managed to get themselves admitted by reporting hallucinations the night before. Thereafter they behaved completely normally and it took an average of 30 days to get discharged. Behaviour which was normal for the researchers (taking notes) was viewed by the staff as bizarre: it was described in the day book as 'engaged in writing behaviour'. The 'patients' who were discharged earliest were those who eventually confessed to having been ill but were now 'feeling better'. Those who continued to profess their normality were kept in the longest as it was believed they were deliberately feigning to get out—clearly pathological behaviour in a mental hospital. (The only people within the hospital to realize the researchers were 'normal' were the other patients!)

Though this study demonstrated the dilemma of appropriate behaviour in a mental hospital it is uncertain whether it substantiates the labelling perspective. One critic has argued it merely shows the diagnostic ineptitude of the admitting psychiatrists. This is probably the significant point. It is only when early mistakes are made in diagnosis that 'normal' patients are exposed to the potentially unsettling experience of being a patient in a psychiatric setting. Yet it can be argued that because psychiatric diagnostic categories are relatively imprecise mistakes can be made. Occasionally a mistake is brought to light by the media but it is impossible without further empirical study to judge the overall impact of this process on the emergence of new psychiatric cases.

c. Psychiatric illness can be exacerbated by labelling and secondary deviance. The evidence to support this hypothesis comes from patients who have been incarcerated for long periods of time in mental hospitals. They manifest behaviour which is appropriate for the inside of a mental hospital but which is incongruous for the world outside. This phenomenon of institutionalization, as discussed earlier, denotes the process by which the inmates of large institutions gradually withdraw from normal life and become wholly dependent.

There is now general awareness of the dangers of prolonged institutionalization and some of these effects can be combatted by minimizing the period of hospitalization and, where hospitalization is necessary, by ensuring a suitable ward environment. One effect of 'therapeutic communities', which almost completely reject traditional ward structure and authority, is to prepare the patient for rapid integration back into the community when sufficiently recovered.

Further reading

Goffman E. 1961
Asylums: Essays on the Social Situation of Mental Patients and Other In-mates. London, Penguin.
   See especially 'On the characteristics of total institutions'.

Goffman E. 1963
Stigma: Notes on the Management of Spoiled Identity. London, Penguin.
   The other classic statement on how identities can be changed through 'secondary deviance'.

Clare A. 1976
Psychiatry in Dissent. London, Tavistock.
   A discussion of controversies in psychiatry including 'labelling' and the nature of psychiatric disorder.

7 *Social factors in disease aetiology*

This chapter ignores the means by which disease labels come to be created and instead examines the social causes of disease.

7.1. Causality

Before proceeding further, some pitfalls in assuming a causal relationship between two variables will be described.

There are three conditions which must be fulfilled for it to be possible to claim that two variables are causally related, e.g. A causes B (A→B).

a. They must occur in the correct *temporal sequence*. The independent variable, A, must precede in time the dependent variable, B: if it does not then their relationship cannot be causal. In the natural sciences discovering the temporal sequence of two variables is not often a serious problem. However, in the behavioural sciences, and especially under non-experimental conditions, it may be difficult. For instance, it may be suggested that a patient became depressed as a result of losing his job, but equally plausible would be the hypothesis that he became depressed and then lost his job through an inability to work properly.

b. There must be a *correlation* between the variables such that as A varies, B varies (A∝B). Usually some statistical test will establish if a correlation exists.

c. There must be *no spurious third variable*. This is the most difficult condition to test for. If a spurious variable exists then the observed change in A and B can be explained by a change in the third variable, S.

For instance, there may be a correlation between the number of television sets and heart attacks:

Number of televisions ∝ heart attacks

However, it is unlikely that one is causing the other. By introducing a third variable, affluence, a more plausible model is produced: affluence causes increased spending on consumer goods and the sale of TVs increases: at the same time affluence produces a change in life style, perhaps in diet, which may increase the heart attack rate.

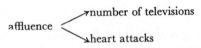

affluence → number of televisions / heart attacks

Thus the apparent relationship between numbers of televisions and heart attacks is explained by the third, spurious variable, affluence.

A more familiar example is that of the relationship between cigarette smoking and lung cancer. There is a well established correlation between these two variables and they occupy the correct temporal sequence (it seems highly unlikely that having lung cancer makes the patient smoke cigarettes). But is the relationship causal?

It has been suggested that it is a personality type which 'causes' both cigarette smoking and cancer. Thus it is possible to construct two different causal models to show the relationship between smoking and lung cancer.

i. smoking   ⟶   cancer

ii. extroversion ⟶ smoking / cancer

In both models there is the correct temporal sequence and both models will show a correlation between smoking and cancer. A test of the latter hypothesis, however, became available when one section of the population (doctors) radically decreased their cigarette consumption after a link between smoking and cancer was first suggested. The result was a decrease in cancer in this group. If model (ii) had been correct then stopping smoking should have had no effect on their cancer rate, since personalities, which supposedly cause the cancer, remained constant.

However, even though in this survey the hypothesized causal relationship between smoking and cancer was confirmed, it does not exclude other spurious variables from being able to refute the relationship. For instance, doctors' cancer rate may have gone down not because they gave up smoking but because they also perhaps became less anxious and it is anxious people who get cancer and who tend to smoke.

In other words, the condition for causality which specifies the absence of a third spurious variable is unattainable. But this does not mean that the hypothesized relationship should be rejected; it is at least now known to be better than believing that extroversion causes cancer. In short the claim of causality is always a provisional one. It is only by successive testing of the relationship against the more obvious and plausible alternatives that increased reliance can be placed on the hypothesis despite its provisional nature.

7.2. The causal sequence

The other problem of establishing causality is that the relationship A→B is really an abstraction from a much larger model. It ignores why A changes and it ignores the possible 'mechanisms' by which A changes B. Thus a more comprehensive model might be:

$$X \rightarrow A \rightarrow Y \rightarrow B$$

A and B are still causally related but so are X and B, and Y and B. The answer to the question 'What causes B?' can be provided in a variety of ways, all different but all correct. Sometimes in medicine competing explanations are merely different selections from the same causal sequence, and whereas for some, A might be the cause of B, for others it is relegated to a part of the mechanisms by which X causes B.

The picture in medicine is further complicated by the fact that disease aetiology cannot justly be represented by such a simple causal sequence; instead a multifactorial model is more appropriate.

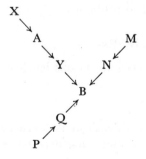

For example, it will be suggested in the next section that social class is incriminated in the aetiology of various diseases such as infection and ischaemic heart disease, yet medical textbooks are more likely to stress bacteria and serum cholesterol levels. How can these two apparently different explanations be reconciled?

Referring to the above discussion there seem to be two possibilities.

a. The cause of the disease is multifactorial. For a patient to develop tuberculosis requires both the presence of the Koch bacillus and a poor nutritional state, which might be a product of social conditions. Hence both factors may be necessary preconditions for developing the disease.

b. The two explanations are taken from different points in the same causal sequence. Thus it may be that:

low	poor	high	ischaemic
social class $\longrightarrow$	diet $\longrightarrow$	serum cholesterol $\longrightarrow$	heart disease

In this sequence, low social class, poor diet and high serum cholesterol can all be said to be causes of ischaemic heart disease. The choice, however, is of more than academic interest for it will affect—

i. the direction of research effort.

ii. the treatment judged appropriate.

Thus, in medicine, when the cause of a disease is identified it represents a choice from a wide selection of possible causal factors, both in type and over time. The contribution of the behavioural sciences to an understanding of disease aetiology is to claim neither that the new explanations of behavioural science are better nor that the more common biological explanations are wrong. The contribution is towards the consideration of a wider selection of causal variables which might help to give a better understanding of disease aetiology, and hence of the nature of, and potential treatments for, medical problems.

7.3. Social factors in disease

These can be considered at various levels of generality.

a. Economic factors

The principal causes of death in Western countries are ischaemic heart disease, cancer and 'degenerative changes'. The major killers in the Third World tend to be infections. These differences are not unique to certain geographical or climatic regions but seem linked to a particular state of economic development. In Britain a hundred years or so ago a similar pattern of mortality was seen; infectious diseases such as tuberculosis, diphtheria, cholera, measles etc., were the principal causes of death, especially in children.

Besides these changes in the actual cause of death, the major change in mortality over the past hundred years in Britain has been a fall in infant mortality. The increase in longevity in adult during this period, by comparison, has been much less dramatic. Thus over the last seventy years life expectancy at birth has increased some 20–25 years, whereas for the middle-aged it has only increased 4–8 years. Moreover these changes, in both causes of death and death rates, occurred before the advent of modern technological medicine with its vast range of chemotherapies. The classical illustration of this is the decline in mortality from tuberculosis which used to be the major cause of death in the nineteenth century. (*Fig.* 1.)

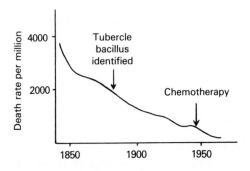

Fig. 1. Respiratory tuberculosis: mean annual death rates. Age standardized. England and Wales. (After McKeown.)

As can be seen from the graph the main fall in mortality occurred well before the discovery of anti-tuberculosis drugs. The cause of this earlier decline is generally attributed to an increasing standard of living which resulted in an improvement in health through better housing, nutrition, etc., and to specific public health measures such as effective sanitation. In short the state of economic development seems to bring in its wake improvements in style of living that are beneficial to health.

That said, it would be wrong to conclude that economic growth is inevitably good for health. It is now arguable that some of the principal health hazards are themselves maintained by the economic system—whether it is affluence which increases the numbers of motor cars and hence road traffic accidents (the commonest cause of death in young people) or the relatively unrestrained consumption of cigarettes (the largest single avoidable cause of death). It is ironic too that every car accident which requires repairs, or every person who needs medical treatment for lung cancer, is contributing to the wealth of the country through being counted in the gross national product (GNP).

Having overcome the diseases of economic under-development it would thus be short-sighted to say that economic factors now play little part in maintaining a certain pattern of disease. Equally it would be wrong to assume a simple relationship and assert that our current problems are diseases of affluence. Even within our society disease and illness still seem to be more prevalent in the lower socio-economic strata: it is not the overworked business man or professional who has the highest rate of heart attacks but the unskilled worker. While the higher mortality experience of the lower social classes is probably due to a number of factors it would be unwise to exclude 'disease of deprivation' from these. The interrelationship between economic factors and health remains a complex one.

b. Cultural factors

Apart from the wide differences in disease patterns as a result of economic development there also appear to be various cultural factors which can affect specific patterns of disease. Japan and the USA, for example, are both relatively affluent societies and have roughly equivalent health status, but there are some specific differences. In Japan cancer of the upper gastro-intestinal tract and cerebrovascular disease are much more common than in the USA whereas in the latter breast cancer and ischaemic heart disease are in turn much more common than in Japan. In answer to the question as to whether this is due to environmental or genetic differences there is evidence to suggest the former. When Japanese emigrate to the USA and adopt the American style of life then disease rates tend to approximate to that of their new host country. However, the specific cultural factors involved in these disease patterns are for the most part unknown.

In trying to discover the reasons for an apparent excess of one disease in a certain country it is sometimes difficult to distinguish between the relative importance of cultural and geographical factors. It might be argued that the high rate of chronic bronchitis in the UK is a product of a relatively damp climate, though the effects of air pollution and smoking—both of social origin— cannot be ignored. Similarly the high incidence of spina bifida in parts of Ireland may be due to some facet of the style of life, e.g. nutrition, pollution or to some contaminant in the natural environment. But though the causal agent might come from the natural environment the range and penetration of the social world often means that the agent is brought into human contact by cultural means. To take a simple example, a disease organism may only be found in one water supply but it is the choice of source, perhaps a river instead of a well, that ultimately determines the disease pattern.

c. Sub-cultural factors

It might be thought that cultural differences of causal significance can only be identified across widely different societies. This is not so. In the UK there are considerable variations between different people in their style of life; perhaps the most important variation in both culture and morbidity/mortality is found between social classes (see Section 3.3).

If the mortality figures of the various social classes are examined large differences are apparent (Table 11). Morbidity is more difficult to measure (see Section 10.2) but is probably similar.

This correlation of health status with social class poses many questions. What exactly is the relationship? What are the factors within the broad term 'social class' that are of aetiological significance?

i. Some may be related, as in the nineteenth century, to poorer housing, nutrition, hygiene, etc., in the lower social classes and these may explain some of their poor health.

ii. Particular behaviour patterns may be related to higher mortality. Working class people tend to under-use preventive services and, in proportion to their morbidity, under-use health services. They also smoke more than middle-class groups: under

Table 11. MORTALITY BY SOCIAL CLASS

Males		Standardized mortality ratios* (1970–72)
Social class	I	77
	II	81
	III	104
	IV	113
	V	137
Mothers		Perinatal mortality† (1973)
Social class	I	15·3
	II	17·1
	III	21·5
	IV	23·5
	V	31·5

* Standardized mortality ratio (SMR) is produced by comparing the actual and expected mortality rates for a group taking into consideration their age distribution. Thus in this column the average is 100.
† Perinatal mortality is the number of stillbirths and deaths in the first week of life per 1000 live and stillbirths.

40% of professional males smoke whereas over 60% of male unskilled manual workers do so.

The mortality differences between social classes are of particular interest because—

—they include many apparently unrelated diseases

—they are found in husbands (whose occupation places their family in its social class) and their wives. Thus it suggests that it is not only occupational diseases (details of which are beyond the scope of this book) but also something about the 'way of life' in the various social classes which leads to this excess of ill-health.

d. Family factors

Support for the significance of the 'way of life' as a causal factor has come from studies of marital status and mortality. The assumption is that if mortality varies by marital status then some aspect of marriage, or non-marriage, itself may be of aetiological importance.

One study in the US compared suicide rates of married and unmarried. (*Table* 12.)

These data suggest that single males, for example, have twice the risk of committing suicide compared with married males, and

Table 12. SUICIDE RATES BY MARITAL STATUS
(Ratios produced by dividing the suicide rate of the unmarried by the rate of the married. Age 25–64.)

Single	male	2·00
	female	1·51
Widowed	male	5·01
	female	2·21
Divorced	male	4·75
	female	3·43

that divorced males have over four times the risk. But whether this risk factor is due to the marital status or to some other factor it is difficult to say. For instance, it might be argued that people who don't get married are 'abnormal' in some way and are therefore more likely to commit suicide. Thus—

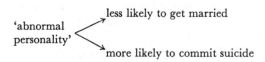

In this example the relationship between marital status and suicide is entirely spurious. A similar argument could be used for divorced people though a different one must be found for widowed (losing a spouse presumably has little relationship with the survivor's personality).

However, it is possible to perform a similar analysis for other causes of death—for being murdered, being killed by a car, dying from cirrhosis of the liver, lung cancer, diabetes and tuberculosis, for example. The risk in all these cases tends to be lower in married people (though not always for women, which might suggest that men get more 'protection' from marriage).

Whether all these differences can be explained by reference to personal characteristics of the single, widowed and divorced population or whether they are a product of some internal dynamic of the family is unknown. They do, however, illustrate potential avenues for research. If a virus or a bacterium was found to have contributed as much to mortality as many of the factors discussed in this section then it would likely have been branded as a major threat to health. Various cultures, lower social class or marital status, however, are not so labelled, and part of the reason can be found in the traditional medical view of the nature of disease, which is discussed in Chapter 8.

7.4. Psychiatric disease

The nature of psychiatric illness has perennially posed a problem in medicine because of the traditional separation of mind and body. While the accepted view of disease as an organic pathology has dominated medical thinking, psychiatric disorder, in which there is no apparent organic pathology, has given rise to a multiplicity of theories of both its nature and cause.

a. Biological theories

Three forms of biological theory in psychiatric disorder can be identified.

i. The first claims that all psychiatric problems constitute a residuum of unexplained organic problems. The classic example usually quoted is that of General Paralysis of the Insane (GPI) which, until the discovery of the syphilitic spirochaete, was treated as a psychiatric disorder. Then, when its organic basis became known, it became a neurological rather than a psychiatric problem. This view holds that ultimately all psychiatric disease will be explained by organic pathology and then transferred to neurology.

ii. The second variant also states that all psychiatric phenomena have a biological/biochemical cause but is less negative about the role of psychiatry. Because these disorders manifest themselves with mental symptomatology then they should be grouped together and treated by psychiatrists.

iii. The third view holds that although all psychiatric illnesses may be found to have a biological/biochemical basis this does not preclude either psychological or social factors from the causal sequence. Thus it may be that—

$$\text{bad housing} \longrightarrow \text{stress} \longrightarrow \text{mono-amine oxidase release}$$
$$\downarrow$$
$$\text{depression}$$

In this sequence there is a biochemical cause for the depression but it is also a mechanism through which psychological and social factors cause the disease. This view is therefore not inconsistent with psychological and social theories of aetiology.

b. Psychological theories

There are very many psychological theories of mental illness which in general reduce mental illness to some problem of maladaptive behaviour. Three main groups of behaviour can be identified.

i. Psychoanalytic/psychodynamic which derive from Freudian ideas about the development of the psyche. Mental illness—in this case mainly the neuroses—is a product of problems in the patient's past, especially childhood.

ii. Theories of self such as the Rogerian or Laingian which similarly attribute psychiatric disorder to inadequate concepts of 'self', though these may be derived from current as well as past interpersonal situations.

iii. Behaviourist, which views psychiatric disease in terms of learned maladaptive behaviour.

These theories share in common the belief that psychiatric disorder is fundamentally a problem of the mind but each group of theories offers different and often conflicting views of how the mind came into this state. All theories tend to stress interpersonal relationships as contributory, but how and when they do so is debated.

While many of these theories would be dismissive of biological theories of psychiatric illness, most would probably acknowledge that biochemical changes do occur but these are in some way a consequence of these various interpersonal relationships. Furthermore, it should be noted that besides offering explanation of the cause of mental illness, they also inevitably offer, whether implicitly or explictly, views of the actual nature of psychiatric disorder and its appropriate treatment.

c. Sociological theories

There are two broad sociological approaches to psychiatric disease.

i. *Labelling*. The first is that of labelling, which has been discussed in Chapter 6. This approach differs significantly from all the others in that whereas they search for aetiological factors in the genesis of psychiatric phenomena, the labelling approach holds that the only important aetiological factor is the very process of selecting out for study these same psychiatric phenomena in the first place. This ascription of a label (through the identification of primary deviance) is reinforced by changed interpersonal relations which produces secondary deviance and a full-blown mental illness.

In as much as this process relies on interpersonal relations for both identification of primary deviance and the emergence of secondary deviance it can be seen that some of the theories of self mentioned above—especially that of Laing—have much in common.

ii. *Social factors.* The other sociological approach, in common with most psychological and biological theories, accepts the existence of psychiatric disorder in its own right irrespective of social labelling. Moreover like other theories of psychiatric disorder the social factor approach emphasises a multifactorial aetiology. In particular, social factors are often divided into those which affect resistance/susceptibility to psychiatric disease and those which can be said to actually trigger it.

Susceptibility/resistance

One of the earliest studies in this field was by the French sociologist Emile Durkheim, at the turn of the century. Durkheim investigated the frequency of suicide in certain European countries, breaking the rates down by various aspects of social structure. For example, he separated the suicide rate of unmarried from married men and women, both with and without children. (*Table* 13.)

He discovered, as is now well established, a greater frequency of suicide among men compared with women, but also he found that both marital status and presence of children seemed to be

Table 13.   SUICIDE RATES BY MARITAL STATUS AND PRESENCE OF CHILDREN

	Suicide rate per *100 000*
Men	
Unmarried men, age 45	975
Husbands with children	336
Husbands without children	644
Women	
Unmarried women, age 42	150
Wives with children	79
Wives without children	221

related to the suicide rate: it seemed that being married and having children was protective.

From these figures Durkheim therefore devised a figure which he called the 'coefficient of preservation'. It was calculated by seeing to what extent married people were less likely to commit suicide. Thus from the figures in *Table* 13, for a married man without children the coefficient is $\frac{975}{644} = 1 \cdot 5$ and for a married man with children it is $\frac{975}{336} = 2 \cdot 9$.

Because each of these numbers is greater than $1 \cdot 0$ it can be seen that marriage seems protective against suicide and furthermore, because the coefficient of the married man with children exceeds that of the married man without children, then the presence of children confers further protection.

The point can be further illustrated if, instead of listing suicide rates, coefficients of preservation are calculated (*Table* 14).

Table 14. SUICIDE RATES EXPRESSED AS 'COEFFICIENT OF PRESERVATION'

	Coefficient of preservation
Men	
Unmarried men, 45 years	$1 \cdot 0$
Husbands with children	$2 \cdot 9$
Husbands without children	$1 \cdot 5$
Women	
Unmarried women, 42 years	$1 \cdot 0$
Wives with children	$1 \cdot 89$
Wives without children	$0 \cdot 67$

From these figures it can be seen that wives with children are protected, as are husbands with children, yet not as much. However, for these women it seems it is the children and not the marriage which is protective, for wives without children are more at risk than unmarried women.

Besides the protective function of marriage and children, Durkheim found that Protestants were more likely to commit suicide than Catholics and Jews. He then went on to try and explain these variations in terms of social integration: the more integrated a person is in a marriage or in a religion then the less likely he is to commit suicide. Several other well established facts, such as the decline of suicide during war-time, would seem to bear this out.

Though this research was completed at the end of the nineteenth century it still seems to hold with more recent data (*Table* 12). Instead of calculating the coefficient of preservation the Table shows the opposite 'coefficient of aggravation' for unmarried people (i.e. when the numbers are greater than 1·0 then the unmarried have that much greater chance of committing suicide).

The study of social factors, especially in the form of social integrators, has also found support in a recent study of depression. There it was found that four factors tended to increase the resistance/susceptibility of a group of women to depression. Women with no outside employment, those with young children at home, especially under 6 years old, those who had lost their mother before the age of 11 and those who had no close confidant were more likely, other things being equal, to have a depressive episode.

Triggers

This same study of depression found that the onset was dependent on a provoking 'life event'. Life events, briefly, were particular stressful events in people's lives such as the death of a close relative, a sudden serious illness, a major car crash, etc.

Life events as triggers of psychiatric disorder have received considerable support from various studies but like much of the research in stress and stressful events many of the studies can be challenged in their design, methods or conclusions. Detailed consideration of these limitations is beyond the scope of this book.

7.5. The limits of aetiology

Knowledge of aetiology is useful in treatment and prevention. If the cause of pneumonia is identified as a certain bacterium, then this can be treated by appropriate antibiotics. Undoubtedly such treatment of cause is better than treatment of symptoms. However, there are certain limitations to this model.

To take a hypothetical causal sequence:

$$\text{bad housing} \longrightarrow \text{stress} \longrightarrow \text{mono-amine oxidase release}$$
$$\downarrow$$
$$\textbf{depression}$$

If the disease is diagnosed as depression the cause could be either seen as housing, stress or an enzyme. Whichever cause is selected will determine treatment: rehousing or psychotherapy or mono-amine oxidase inhibitors may be appropriate treatments. The selection will tend to depend on two factors:

a. availability/practicality.

b. the doctor's particular bias.

The availability of treatment will depend on current technology and also on the doctor's bias as this will in the long term influence research. For example, the search for a 'cure' for lung cancer in the form of biomedical research takes perhaps a hundred times the resources that are devoted to prevention. Thus in the sequence

$$smoking \longrightarrow histological\ change \longrightarrow lung\ cancer$$

the locus of cause and hence treatment tends to be the biological change rather than the social habit. The concept of aetiology, in that it involves selection from preceding and concurrent causal influences, will rarely offer more than just a partial picture of the patient's world. It may in turn constrain the doctor's perception of possible treatments. Prevention, for example, has received relatively little attention from researchers.

The second limit to aetiology is that it assumes that disease is static: causal factors lead to a specific disease end-point. Such a model may be useful in sharply defined illnesses such as many acute diseases, but is more limited in helping with chronic or less specific complaints. Here both 'cause' and 'disease' may be on-going processes which interact. Thus in a patient presenting with both depression and an exacerbation of a chronic osteo-arthrosis it may be impossible to distinguish causal factors between the two. In many patients a collection of problems may co-exist and be mutually supporting.

Further reading

McKeown T. 1976
The Role of Medicine: Dream, Mirage or Nemesis? London, Nuffield.

A summary of his findings on the relative contributions of social and chemotherapeutic measures on mortality over the last 100 years or so.

Brown G. W. and Harris T. 1979
Social Origins of Depression. London, Tavistock.
A report on the link between life events and depression. Also a good summary of methodological problems.

8 *Doctor, patient and problem*

In the previous chapter the medical problem has been equated with disease. This chapter examines the medical problem in a wider context.

Undoubtedly the concept of disease is a mainstay of the hospital definition of what constitutes the medical problem though outside, in general practice, the concept has more limited utility. Chapter 2, on why people go to the doctor, served to show the variety of reasons a patient might have for visiting the doctor which, though they may involve 'organic' symptoms, cannot be identified and managed out of the context of the patient's psychological state and social environment.

A second reason for discussing the nature of the 'problem' in medicine is for the light it can throw on doctor–patient and interprofessional relationships. Team work might be in fashion but the value of the health care team is unlikely to be great if, for instance, the team members cannot agree on what the problem is or on who should be treating it.

Finally, certain issues raised by the extension of the purview of medicine from discrete organic diseases to wider social issues will be discussed.

8.1. Identifying the medical problem

In the preceding chapter it was suggested that the aetiology of lung cancer might be described as:

$$\underbrace{\text{smoking} \longrightarrow \text{histological change}}_{\text{aetiology}} \longrightarrow \underbrace{\text{lung cancer}}_{\text{problem}}$$

In this formulation smoking and/or histological change can be viewed as the cause of the disease. Furthermore in this example the disease, lung cancer, constitutes the medical problem in which the doctor is ultimately interested.

But of course the sequence does not stop with lung cancer. There are also the consequences or outcomes of the disease. Thus:

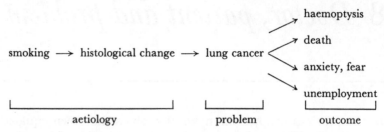

These outcomes will vary in type—some biological, some psychological, some social—and they will vary over time.

This model can further be increased in comprehensiveness if some of the arguments in the preceding chapter on aetiology are considered. The diagram should take account of the fact that—

i. Smoking itself is part of a longer causal sequence:

e.g. stress ⟶ smoking.

ii. Smoking is a part of other causal sequences:

e.g. smoking ⟶ chronic bronchitis.

iii. The cause of lung cancer is undoubtedly multifactorial:

Adding these to the model:

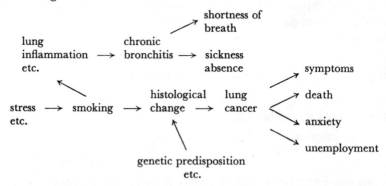

Clearly this process of adding more variables could continue almost indefinitely but for present purposes it is sufficient to take this particular model.

What now is the medical problem? With a more simple sequence it was possible to describe the lung cancer as the problem, but this can now be seen as a somewhat crude abstraction. Smoking has as much claim to be the 'real' problem as has lung cancer or chronic bronchitis. In effect there is no such thing as a 'real' problem and the variables that are selected from the potential range to constitute the problem are a function of the beliefs of the selector. Consider some of the various people and agencies which might be involved in identifying the problem.

a. The *government/community* may claim the problem is smoking because if intervention is directed at this point many of the consequences would not occur and later expensive treatment would be averted.

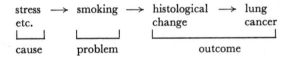

Equally the government might be concerned at the sickness absence rate or the level of unemployment due to sickness, in which case the problem is located elsewhere.

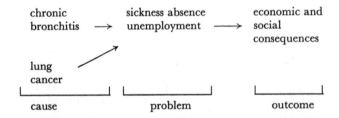

b. The *medical profession* has traditionally tended to emphasise diseases as the core of the medical problem.

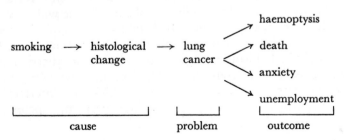

This emphasis on disease states and entities has historical roots which are beyond the scope of this book. The disease model, however, provides a useful method of classifying problems. Identifying the problem as lung cancer, though, does not necessarily improve the effectiveness of treatment: in this case 'treatment' would be far better directed at smoking.

The disease model is merely one of potentially many ways of classifying medical problems. Its advantage lies in the fact that in its long history it has been considerably refined and developed and so now provides a fairly sophisticated means of classifying problems which in turn enables treatment to be appropriately directed.

The disadvantage with this model is that over-adherence to a rigid classification can cause important factors which do not fall into the classification to be overlooked. There is a tendency to reduce the cause of the disease to pathology of anatomy, physiology or biochemistry and to limit outcome to similar biological parameters. Thus:

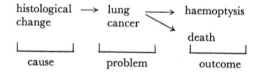

The emphasis on micro-biological cause reflects the nature of the problem classification. The emphasis on biological outcomes reflects both the need to identify biological symptoms (e.g. haemoptysis) as a means of classifying the disease in the first place and on biological consequences as a way of assessing the course and history of the (biologically defined) problem. In certain situations such biases are undoubtedly justified. In others they serve to limit the doctor's potential range of effectiveness.

c. Finally the *patient* too defines problems. These will vary over time. Initially the symptoms which first present will be seen as the problem. (It is of interest that the conception of medical problems which historically preceded that of localized organic pathology was a rigorous classification of all symptoms.) Symptoms will be recognized to the extent to which they interfere with normal routine, and advice will be sought from the doctor as to their nature and cause. (*See* Section 2.2.)

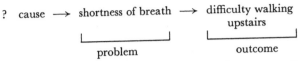

When the doctor has given the diagnosis in terms of, say, bronchitis or lung cancer then the patient too might see the problem in disease terms. However, the psychological and social consequences of that disease process will always remain both the justification for acceptance of a medical diagnosis and an important part of the total problem. In this sense the 'problem' tends to merge with its cause and its consequences: all are part of the overall patient's problem.

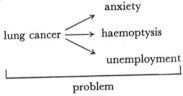

The medical problem thus becomes a multiplicity of smaller problems which are themselves inextricably intertwined with the patient's own biography, personality and environment. The meaning and implications of lung cancer for a 70-year-old retired civil servant will be different from those of a 35-year-old housewife. The extent to which anxiety and fear are problems will vary according to the patient, as will reaction to haemoptysis or unemployment.

In the final analysis, when the limits of the medical problem have been extended, every patient presents a unique problem of management. Classification, whether it is by diagnostic categories, personality types or social class, can be a useful adjunct to the management of the problem but any of these taken in isolation might only serve to emphasise a part of what, to the patient, constitutes a totality.

The implications of this for the doctor's work are now explored.

8.2. The medical task

In view of the preceding discussion the exact definition of the medical task can be seen as very difficult. It will vary from doctor to doctor, from health professional to health professional, from specialist to specialist and from situation to situation.

The potential range of the medical problem can be illustrated with two cases.

a. The surgeon

If a patient presents with an acute abdomen the value of an accurate diagnosis is self-evident for without it the surgeon may not offer the appropriate treatment. In this case, from signs and symptoms, the surgeon reaches a diagnosis—couched in terms of pathology within the abdomen—which requires treatment. Other factors may be considered in deciding on treatment such as the patient's age or general health but in essence these other points neither add nor subtract from the specific biological character of the clinical diagnosis. The organic pathology remains in all probability the central medical problem at that moment whatever the other factors.

b. The general practitioner

Now consider the same patient six months later following partial gastrectomy for perforated peptic ulcer: the patient presents to the GP with vague abdominal pains. Like the surgeon before him the GP must consider whether these symptoms have an organic basis, either in further gastric ulceration or as some unpleasant sequelae of the operation.

The patient is no longer a semi-comatose passive body in which the most over-riding problem is the life-threatening peritonitis. Thus, the GP might also discover from the patient's notes or the interview that the patient's mother died from stomach cancer, and that the patient's marriage has recently entered a difficult period.

The problem can now be transformed according to how these three areas—the abdominal pains, the mother's death and the marital discord—are handled. Are they simply three independent problem areas? Or are the pains an indication of the patient's anxiety about possible cancer? Or a consequence of the marital discord?

The medical problems here can be considered to be (i) only the abdominal pain and the other matters of no concern to the doctor, or (ii) as multi-faceted and all areas require consideration and possibly treatment.

a. The difficulty with adopting this approach is that even if organic pathology is considered the sole subject matter of medicine, its identification and treatment will be the poorer if other psycho-social phenomena are not considered. It may be justified to ignore the latter when the patient is entirely passive but these situations, such as when the patient is under anaesthesia in the operating theatre, are relatively rare. In this situation it matters little whether the patient has six children at home or is depressed, but immediately after the operation these biographical details may become important.

Even if the medical task is viewed primarily as the identification and treatment of organic disease some consideration of psycho-social factors remains important in certain parts of clinical practice.

—A useful clinical history is dependent on establishing a good rapport with the patient. This requires certain social skills to put patients at their ease.

—Patient compliance with treatment requires consideration of psycho-social factors. Treatment of a disease is clearly inadequate if the patient does not follow the treatment. Up to 20% of prescriptions are never presented to the pharmacist and perhaps one-third of drugs prescribed are not taken. Did the patient understand the instructions? Do they know why they must take the treatment? Have they been warned about side-effects? If good patient compliance is to be established then the patient's attitudes and beliefs must be considered as well as the specific 'pathology'.

—Avoidance of unnecessary treatment requires consideration of psycho-social factors. Many patients with psycho-social problems present to the doctor with 'organic' complaints (*see* next section). If the psycho-social problem is not 'excluded' then unnecessary treatment, perhaps with unwanted side-effects, might be given. A large proportion of patients on medical and surgical wards have some emotional problem. This might be as a consequence of their organic problem; it might be because emotional and organic problems tend to 'cluster' in people's lives; or it might be because a patient with psycho-social problems is being unnecessarily investigated and treated, with all that entails in terms of cost, inconvenience and side-effects. At the very least, psycho-social problems which might have led to the original presentation of some 'organic' symptomatology must be excluded.

b. On the other hand the medical problem can be defined as also existing in the patient's biography and environment. From the discussion in Chapter 4 on the nature of disease it is clear that disease is a phenomenon that interferes with social functioning. Thus if a patient has bronchitis the problem might be shortness of breath while climbing stairs or if rheumatoid arthritis, difficulty in washing-up or if varicose veins, pain on standing, etc. While the specific organic diagnosis may give some guidance as to the cause, the problem itself is firmly rooted in the patient's life and other aspects of that life become relevant to a full understanding.

One difficulty with this approach is in knowing its limits. Many biographical details may seem completely irrelevant to whatever is identified as the main problem. Secondly, for many of them no help or advice can usefully be given and thirdly, when adopting this wider approach, the doctor can be charged with 'medicalizing' more aspects of everyday life. (*See* Section 8.4.)

On balance the limits of the doctor's definition of the medical problem must be decided in the context of the problem with which the patient presents. Whatever the doctor's skills or involvement with the case the problem is ultimately the patient's.

8.3. The doctor's interpretation of symptoms

a. Organic symptoms

These are the commonest presenting symptoms and may be indicative of specific organic pathology. They also involve the doctor considering psycho-social aspects in two ways:

i. Organic symptoms may present as a 'cover' for some psycho-social problem. Many patients feel it inappropriate to bring a psycho-social problem directly to the doctor as it is thought the doctor may not be interested or that it is an admission of weakness or failure. In such a case, organic symptomatology, which is a fairly routine occurrence, can act as a ticket to gain access to the doctor.

Though the connection between psychological problem and presenting symptom may be consciously held by the patient (i.e. the organic symptom is used explicitly as a 'ticket'), for some patients the connection may be less apparent. Indeed the patient may, for instance, present with increasingly severe migraine attacks yet never have thought there might be some relationship with moving house or an ill child at home.

ii. Even when psycho-social factors are not overtly a part of the presenting symptomatology they nevertheless intrude in all organic diseases. The patient with a heart attack, with a cold, with appendicitis or with eczema, also has a life and experience beyond the particular pathology which will inevitably influence the response to the disease and treatment. Work, leisure, marriage, children, etc., constitute the context of every illness and in the final analysis the patient is not concerned with the pathology itself but with its effect both now and in the future, on these activities and experiences. One of the doctor's tasks is to treat organic pathology so that it will have minimal impact on the patient's life, but this emphasis on the biological as the field of action need not deter the doctor from recognizing that the patient has worries and concerns of a different emphasis despite working towards similar goals.

b. *Psychological symptoms*

Variation in psychological state may well be normal and quite acceptable for the patient. There is probably wide personal and social variation in mood swings and whether help is sought for, say, a depressive episode will be a function of the individual threshold and ability to cope.

When the symptoms are judged severe enough to merit advice then the patient may turn to the doctor. There is some evidence that a reluctance to see this type of symptom as a legitimate medical problem is changing and more people seem willing to seek the doctor's advice. However, there is also, especially for mental problems, a wide range of lay contacts who, the patient may believe, have as great if not greater skills than the doctor: family, close friends and clergymen have traditionally been supports in this area.

When psychological symptoms are presented to the doctor they may be variously interpreted. Of crucial importance here is the particular theory of mental functioning and human behaviour that the doctor accepts. (*See* Section 7.4.) There are, however, several overall interpretations the doctor can use.

i. The psychological symptom may signify an underlying organic pathological process. There may be a direct connection in which brain pathology, e.g. vitamin deficiency, brain tumour, haemorrhage, etc., manifests itself in some change in behaviour or psychological function. Or there may be an indirect connection in which, though the fundamental problem is some organic process, the patient for a variety of reasons presents with psychological symptoms. Thus the patient may present with an anxiety state through worrying that the blood passed per rectum signified a bowel cancer.

ii. The psychological symptom may signify psychiatric disorder. The exact relationship will again be a function of the particular theory employed but the main feature of this perception is that the symptom itself lies at the core of the problem. Concomitant organic problems which emerge, e.g. headache, may themselves be a product of the psychological problem (hence 'psycho-somatic' disease).

iii. The psychological symptom may be a response to an intolerable social situation.

The fact that social, psychological and organic problems are so intermeshed means that the interpretation of presenting symptoms may be a complex process. Indeed, the doctor may never arrive at a clear idea of their mutual relationship but instead must assign priority as best he can, based on both the patient's actual history and the availability of effective therapeutic measures.

8.4. The doctor–patient relationship

Various studies of the doctor–patient relationship—particularly by social psychologists—have stressed the importance of communication skills in 'improving' the relationship. Clearer explanations, more empathy, the ability to listen, etc., have all been suggested as important dimensions of a successful consultation. Yet perhaps of greater importance is the context in which the communication takes place.

Neither doctor nor patient enter the consultation as 'neutral' beings willing to negotiate on all points; instead they enter with certain goals and interests which will dictate the form of the interaction. Some of the goals of the patient have been outlined in Chapter 2 and the patient's approach to the interaction, and the communication within it, will inevitably reflect these particular interests.

The doctor, on the other hand, as has been outlined in the previous two sections, will approach the patient according to how the nature of the problem is defined. In emergency surgery the niceties of full explanations and discussion of the patient's home life may be quite irrelevant to the problem at hand. Alternatively, if the doctor believes a marital difficulty is at the root of the patient's problem then the situation demands a more painstaking and sensitive interview. In short, it is the way the doctor defines the problem which will be the prime determinant of the form and quality of the communication with the patient. Communication skills may of course help the doctor achieve these ends but of themselves can do little to change the form of the interaction if, for example, the doctor is narrowly intent on uncovering specific organic pathology with minimal consideration of the patient as a person.

Similarly, when different members of the health team are called upon to work together, how they do so will very much depend on how they define the problem they are supposed to be tackling. Paediatrician, GP, health visitor, nurse and social worker might all want to help the 'battered baby'. But what is the problem that requires attention? The injuries? The parents? The home life? The future risks? Which is the most important problem and what is the best way of managing it?

When a specific goal is mutually accepted (perhaps to remove an appendix) and an appropriate division of labour organized (anaesthetist, surgeon, theatre nurse, etc.) then the health team can be expected to work smoothly and efficiently. When, however, there is no such agreement on goals nor on specific roles then conflict is likely to arise. As in the doctor–patient relationship, communication skills can be of benefit in working as a team, but if fundamental disagreements exist on the nature of the problem then tensions can result whatever the personal qualities and wishes of the health personnel involved. Particular skills and tolerance do not necessarily constitute a panacea for conflicts which are rooted in the way the medical problem is defined. Moreover, although such conflict can be stressful and difficult for members of the health care team it may also be in the patient's interests that these issues are widely discussed, and perhaps fought over, rather than being reduced to a bland consensus by the health professionals against which the patient has little room to present his perception of the problem.

8.5. Medicalization

As was pointed out in the previous discussion the traditional definition of a medical problem as a biological entity has changed considerably. Psychological and social variables have now come to play an important part in medicine and this change has mostly been welcomed in that it offers a more comprehensive management of health problems in their widest sense.

However, that said, there are critics of this involvement of medicine in new areas. They hold that this process of 'medicalization' has invaded people's lives to an unwarranted degree and now medicine, through this new imperialism, has become a major and potentially dangerous social and political power.

The arguments of these critics can roughly be divided into two—though they are inter-related. Both these arguments will be briefly summarized and then set in context.

a. Medicine as a new source of morality

In two major areas, it is claimed, medicine has invaded areas which were once the province of the individual or of individual responsibility.

The first of these is the notion of responsibility itself. It has been argued that medicine has taken responsibility from the individual and vested it in abstract notions of disease and mental illness. Thus a man is held responsible for a murder that he committed until medicine intervenes to declare him insane; or a woman is held responsible for a bout of shoplifting until medicine 'explains' her behaviour with reference to hormonal disturbance.

Especially through psychiatry, medicine is now invading areas of human behaviour to claim that it alone has a full explanation and therefore legitimate jurisdiction over them. The corollary of this is that the social deviant increasingly falls into the hands of medicine for treatment/punishment.

The second area in which medicine affects people's lives is in its legislation of what is 'good' for healthy living. It is argued that as preventive medicine has incriminated many habits such as smoking, drinking alcohol, eating certain foods, not taking exercise, etc., as conducive to ill-health this in some ways justifies medicine, either on its own or through the State, intervening in people's lives when they are apparently healthy on the pretext of keeping them that way. The 'authorities' might condemn some habits or fashions to little avail until they can be labelled as health hazards. Then intervention to prevent them from occurring seems morally justified.

These two arguments have found much support especially from some psychiatrists, such as Szasz (*see* Section 6.5), who believe medicine is used to justify behaviour control. They can point to the very large quantities of psychotropic drugs consumed to control patients' moods, to hypnotics to control their sleep, to medical treatments of violent criminals and sexual offenders, and so on. A particularly salient example might be the incarceration in mental hospitals of political and social dissidents in some countries.

However, although these arguments might be basically correct —medicine may be increasing its control over social behaviour— medicine always has been an institution of social control rivalling that of the church and of the law. (*See* Chapter 5.) The force of the argument is therefore substantially weakened. Through diagnosis, whether organic or psychiatric, medicine always has been a major influence on social values and behaviour. Its extension in recent years merely reflects a realignment between the church, the law and medicine.

Whether the medicalization of aspects of everyday life is necessarily 'undesirable' is therefore open to debate. Ultimately it revolves around the degree of responsibility individuals are both held to possess and believed should possess. Is the smoker responsible for his folly and therefore accountable (whatever the theories of addiction that medicine might suggest) or is the smoker an unwitting pawn in the hands of an advertising and industrial complex which offers little choice on whether or not to smoke? As so often in medicine it comes down to political beliefs.

b. Medicine as a creator of ill-health

The charge that medicine actually creates ill-health has been cogently argued by Illich. Briefly his argument, so far as medicalization goes, is that by offering a wide range of supportive services for all kinds of unpleasant symptoms medicine has gradually made the patient dependent on the doctor to cope with everyday life. Because the doctor is willing and ready to prescribe analgesics for minor headaches or offer a listening ear to a personal crisis, patients are not required to come to terms with these problems themselves. Thus, Illich argues, people's ability to tolerate pain is lessened, their capacity to cope with life's trials is weakened and like an addict they gradually become wholly dependent on the doctor for more and more minor complaints. The doctor therefore, like the drug pusher, is actually generating the problem he is purporting to solve.

Illich is undoubtedly right to condemn medicine when it equates health in some way with the consumption of medical resources. When he argues that 'death is the ultimate in consumer resistance' he is stating graphically that much of high technology medicine, especially in terminal illness, is orientated towards consumption like many other products of an industrialized society, rather than towards health.

The problem with his argument appears when the alternative vision of health he is offering is considered. For Illich, independence is an integral component of health and therefore dependency, especially on the doctor, constitutes ill-health. In effect the power of Illich's argument lies in his sleight of hand in promoting general acceptance of his definition of health.

To what extent, however, are health and dependency contradictory? Is dependency so undesirable? Again the argument returns to politics because Illich is offering a political view of how he thinks people should be. If a full and healthy life is to be equated with complete personal independence then Illich's indictment of the effects of modern medicine must be broadly correct. However, if dependence on other people whether for services, goods, advice or support is held to be an inevitable consequence of living an ordinary life in a complex society then reliance on the doctor when problems arise is a legitimate and acceptable way of behaving. Whether that reliance/dependence can become too great is not an issue which can be resolved by looking for the 'facts' rather it is a value judgement on the nature of man and the basis of health.

Further reading

Balint M. 1957
The Doctor, his Patient and the Illness. London, Pitman.

A classic book arguing that the medical problem was as much located in the psychosocial domain as in the organic.

Cartwright A. 1967
Patients and their Doctor. London, Routledge & Kegan Paul.
A study of patients, doctors, their perception of each other and their perception of the medical problem.

Illich I. 1975
Medical Nemesis. London, Calder & Boyars.
A polemic against the further medicalization of life.

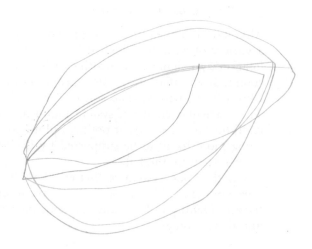

9 *The health care system*

This chapter examines aspects of health care in its wider context. It does not describe in detail the structure and functioning of a health care system in any one country but rather focuses on the sorts of problems encountered by most health services. This should prevent the reader from taking a too parochial view of health care and instead see problems in their proper context.

As in previous chapters the central theme of the discussion is the various meanings placed on the terms health and health need for these are issues which intrude into the administration of a whole health care system just as much as they shape the doctor–patient relationship. A correspondence will be seen between a certain view of health and a particular administrative structure; in some cases this arises as a consequence of deliberately trying to meet a defined health need, in other cases, health services are apparently organized on other criteria but nevertheless involve commensurate implicit or explicit definitions of health.

9.1. Providing health care

Although some health care is provided by all countries there are a variety of ways by which it is 'delivered'. These range from a 'market' system in which health care is treated as any other private commodity to that of complete provision by the State to all those who need it, with various forms of health insurance in between. The particular choice of system found in a country reflects both its history and its current political philosophy, the market system being more likely to be supported by the political right and the State system by the left.

Whether one system is 'better' than the other is a political question which this section does not try to answer. Instead it will try and identify in both these systems their respective advantages and disadvantages.

a. *The market system*

The market system can be illustrated in terms of classical supply and demand curves. (*Fig. 2.*)

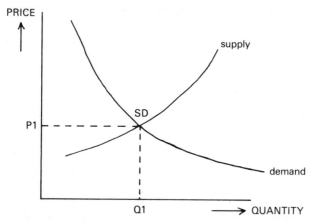

Fig. 2. Market system: supply and demand curves.

In a completely unconstrained market system two curves can be drawn: the supply curve and the demand curve. Briefly, the supply curve shows that as the price of goods rises then the supplier is willing to supply a greater quantity (as he will make more profit), while the demand curve shows that as the price rises the consumer tends to buy less goods (he can't afford them).

By drawing these curves on the same graph they are seen to intersect at the point SD: at this position supply and demand are in equilibrium. This means that producers and consumers can reach an agreement through the market on the price and quantity of goods demanded and supplied. At the point SD the producer is willing to supply goods Q_1 at price P_1 and the consumer is willing to buy goods Q_1 at price P_1. Any other price or quantity would leave either producer or consumer dissatisfied.

This constitutes the chief virtue of the market system in that equilibrium should be reached automatically and the consumers are supposedly 'sovereign' because they can make the free choice whether or not to buy or perhaps whether to buy a substitute instead. Thus in terms of buying health care governments do not have the problem of worrying about how much to provide to meet people's needs as this will be determined in the market by patients who will choose the amount and quantity they want. In short the key theoretical advantage of this system is that a major role is given to the consumer's, i.e. the patient's, view of what is health.

There are, however, several disadvantages to this sort of system. The most important:

i. *The problem of access:* the only patients with free choice, and indeed health care, in this system are those who can afford it. As the greatest need (from the doctor's stand-point) is often found among those with the least money—chronically ill people who may lose their jobs, poor people who are exposed to a more hazardous environment, etc.—then this system tends to allocate health care inappropriately.

Various solutions to overcome this problem have been attempted, the most common being some sort of insurance for those who in ordinary circumstances would not be able to afford care. However, unless the insurance covers all those who may need it and all the treatment they may obtain, it fails to fully compensate for the failing of the market system. On the other hand, the more comprehensive the insurance coverage then the more insurance organizations replace the consumer in evaluating health need, thereby reducing one of the key benefits of the market system.

ii. *The problem of medical monopoly:* the medical profession in developed countries has usually been given a monopoly to supply medical services. Whatever the basis of this monopoly it is usually held to be in the public interest in as much as it prevents unqualified and incompetent practitioners from offering poor or dangerous services to the patient. This monopoly, however, is not consistent with the supply and demand model described as this depends on competition among suppliers to work effectively. A monopoly supplier is able through its monopoly position to artificially force up prices.

The net effect of this is seen in countries in which a market system operates. There is rarely an unconstrained competitive market for, say, surgical operations in which surgeons vie with each other for patients, rather a price is 'recommended' by a professional body and even advertising is usually forbidden. The result may be exploitation of the consumer and, if the government underwrites medical fees through an insurance scheme, rapidly escalating costs.

iii. *The problem of consumer knowledge:* the choice given the consumer in the free market system leaves the consumer to evaluate the quality of health care received. But buying health care is not like buying vegetables. At the supermarket the consumer knows what is wanted and if a mistake is made in choosing very little is lost. In health care, however, consumers may not know exactly what the problem is let alone what is needed; because of this they are often unable to evaluate the quality of care received and moreover, given the nature of the service being bought, a 'mistake' may be disastrous in its consequences. Thus the virtue of consumer choice in the free-market system is seriously tested by their lack of full knowledge (and the general mystification surrounding many of the specialist services offered) and to what extent health demands and wants—which the market caters for—are equivalent to health needs.

iv. *The problem of public health:* while it may seem reasonable to leave the choice of most health services to the consumer's wishes there are some which require government intervention. These relate primarily to public health measures where individual citizens in choosing not to 'buy' the service may endanger not only their own lives (which they are presumably free to do) but also the lives of others. Thus certain measures such as immunization, refuse collection, food inspection, etc., benefit the whole community as well as the individual.

The result of these various problems is that a wholly unconstrained market system for health care does not exist as such in any of the major industrial countries. Most provide a mixture of health care delivery systems. Even when the basis is the private market all countries provide some public health services and to varying degrees some sort of health insurance or State provision for those unable to afford the full cost of a private system.

b. The 'free' State-provided system

Both the advantage and disadvantage of a 'State-provided' system (or 'socialized medicine'), as is the bulk of the British National Health Service, is that the 'need' for health care is separated from 'demand' and the ability to pay. In essence health care is provided for those who need it rather than for those who can afford it, by paying for it through general taxation and making it free at the point of delivery. The problem however is how that need is defined. In the market system need was equated with the wants of the patient, in the State system there is no such mechanism for allocating resources, and criteria other than patient wishes have to be used to establish health need. The problem of defining this need is discussed in the next section.

i. *Priorities*. A further consequence of not having a self-adjusting system for allocating health resources is that decisions have to be taken by government, by hospitals, by doctors, etc., on how much money to spend on health and in what specific areas to spend it. In a market system the amount of resources spent on health is the sum of the choices of individual patients and the amount on different areas—between north and south or between geriatrics and surgery—is determined in exactly the same way. This system is arguably unfair and suffers from the disadvantages already discussed, but it is easier to operate as there are few formal decisions to be taken by administrators or government.

In the State system on the other hand almost all the decisions tend to be taken by administrative bodies. Thus whether the government should spend 5% or 6% of the Gross National Product on health is not answered through some simple mathematical formula. Whether the health service 'needs' more or less money will depend on views as to whether it has too little or too much already and on whether the resources would be better spent on housing, roads, education, etc. Clearly the question of the relative importance of a new school, a new road or a new hospital will depend on the social values of the policy maker.

Similarly it is difficult to compare the value of a new surgical ward against that of a new geriatric ward. Using mortality as an indicator may suggest one is of more value whereas using 'human happiness' it may be the other. Agreement or disagreement with a decision on priorities is therefore an agreement or disagreement on social values, on what constitutes good health and on what importance should be attached to it relative to other states.

ii. *Rationing*. Another problem with the free system is that when the government decides that so much money will be allocated to provide services it is offering a fixed quantity of services, Q_2, to meet a demand which is flexible and potentially greater. (*Fig.* 3.)

Potential demand (the shaded area) would be cut off in the market system by the price, P_2, which would dissuade patients from using more health services. But in the free State system there

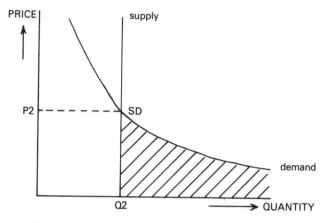

Fig. 3. State intervention: supply and demand curves.

is no financial mechanism by which to limit demand to the quantity of services supplied. This excess demand therefore tends to result in queues and waiting lists.

In effect the price, P_2, necessary to equate demand with supply is paid through non-financial costs such as waiting and inconvenience. These social costs will act as a disincentive to use the service in the same way as would a financial charge.

The main claims of the free service, that it is fair in that it provides health care when and where it is needed, therefore requires some qualification. It is fair in that the rationing mechanism is not dependent on the financial resources of the patient but it can be said to favour instead those who are willing or able to pay the necessary social costs such as inconvenience and waiting. The system, for example, might favour the old-age pensioner as against the busy housewife or the unemployed compared with those in full-time employment. Often those who are unable or unwilling to pay these social costs are better able to pay financial costs and it is therefore not surprising that a private market health system remains viable even alongside a supposedly free State system.

In part the problem of rationing by social cost can be overcome by some 'rational' formula for allocating resources. Thus a 'queue' for renal dialysis can be replaced by a formula which gives priority to certain groups such as the young, those with dependents, etc. Undoubtedly within a free State system there is selection on these sorts of grounds by clinicians, particularly in referral patterns. Whereas in the market system the consumer has a strong say in establishing his need (through expressing demand) in the free State system this task tends to be undertaken by the medical profession, in giving one patient priority over another, and by the government which attempts to direct resources to those parts of the health service with the greatest apparent need.

It is, however, the definition of health need which provides one of the greatest problems of the free State service. Has a chronic arthritic a greater need than a chronic bronchitic? Or has geriatrics a greater need than obstetrics, or the north of the country compared with the south? Questions which are not even considered by the pure market system become crucial if the government is providing the service directly. Some of the issues raised by these questions are discussed in the next section.

9.2. Health need

In allocating resources to different parts of a health service a government may be entirely arbitrary, it may follow historical precedent or it may attempt some 'rational' formula to direct resources towards health needs. If this latter course is adopted then some means must be established of identifying need.

It has been argued in earlier chapters that what constitutes health (and by implication health need) is not an objective judgement but is dependent on who defines it. Using this approach there are broadly three ways of identifying needs. They are: (a) Patient-expressed need. (b) 'Normative' or professionally defined need. (c) Comparative need.

a. Patient-expressed need

As was pointed out in the previous section, patient-expressed need is the basis for the market system of delivering care. The advantage of considering it as a potential means of allocating resource in a free State system is that otherwise patients, and therefore their way of defining health, are unrepresented in the service. While patients may not have all the knowledge necessary to fully judge their own need they still have an important part to play in its identification. Means by which patient-expressed need can be harnessed in a State-provided health care system are several.

i. In the consultation patients have a forum in which to present their own perceptions of their health needs though these are often deferred to those of the doctor.

ii. In management arrangements for actually running a health service the 'patient', through representative bodies, can be given an advisory or executive role to ensure that the health service is meeting what they see as their needs. Problems of adequate 'representativeness' and of conflicts with administrators however can occur. (*See* Section 9.4.)

iii. In identification of priorities the patient plays an indirect role via the electoral process. Inevitably, however, when voting for a candidate or party, voters are not only selecting a particular health policy but a set of policies in other areas. They may find themselves therefore voting for health policies with which they are not in direct accord.

The other means of enabling people's views to be taken into account is by taking surveys of opinion or, given that opinion may be a very tentative measure of need, surveying people's own rating of their health and allocating resources accordingly to those areas with the highest self-reported morbidity. The disadvantage with this latter process is that self-reported morbidity will vary according to the willingness of people to tolerate or report illness and incapacity. Thus if it were used to compare different areas and allocate resources to the area with highest reported morbidity it might be that this area has the lowest morbidity by any other criteria but the most 'complaining' population.

b. Doctor-defined need

The traditional role of the doctor is to define his patient's need. The patient may express various wishes and supposed needs but ultimately doctors must define the 'real' need because of their specialized knowledge. Thus doctor-defined need lies at the heart of clinical practice.

Its advantage is that by allowing the doctor to identify need due deference is given to medical expertise. In certain clinical situations such as emergency surgery there is little doubt of the benefits in permitting the doctor a major role in identifying need. In other situations however, perhaps in the majority of doctor–

patient encounters, the doctor's dominance needs to be tempered by some recognition of the patient's view of the problem and of the particular needs arising from it. The immediate clinical problem is very rarely a life threatening biological lesion but usually involves the psycho-social dimension of the patient's life, and while the doctor may be duly sensitive to this part of the problem, only the patient who lives through it can be aware of many of its details. (*See* Chapter 8.)

The second problem with using a wholly medically defined conception of need is that this assessment is only appropriate to individual patients. Translating this conception to a population therefore tends to be a process of summarizing each of these individual needs. The needs of the population for the doctor are couched in terms of either caseload (how many patients are having treatment) or of population morbidity (how many patients in the community need treatment). While these two measures may indicate something of the need facing an individual clinician they are not so useful when actually allocating resources for neither is easily amenable to comparison across areas, as is discussed below.

c. Comparative need

Comparative need is primarily an administrative device to enable resources to be allocated with some equity between areas (geographical, speciality, diagnostic category, etc.). There are four main indicators which can be used, all of which have advantages and disadvantages.

i. *Morbidity.* Measuring the morbidity in two geographical areas would seem a useful way of comparing their relative need for health care resources. There are, however, two problems which make morbidity a poor indicator of health need.

—Measurement: Whereas in the clinical situation it is often easy to assign diagnoses, in community/epidemiological studies more precise measures have to be used. At what level does diabetes exist? What exactly is chronic bronchitis? etc. These questions make community studies of morbidity particularly difficult and expensive to undertake.

—Comparability: Even if morbidity is accurately measured there are still problems of comparability. Take, for example, the morbidity in two hypothetical regions, A and B.

Number of cases	Region A	Region B
chronic bronchitis	394	241
angina	41	39
osteoarthrosis	204	631
cancers	12	25

Which region has the greater need for health services? The answer is not apparent from the figures because of the difficulty of equating one diagnostic group with another.

The effect of these problems is to restrict the usefulness of morbidity surveys as indicators of need to particular diagnostic/patient groups, e.g. the relative need for treatment for diabetics between areas.

ii. *Mortality.* Mortality rates overcome some of the disadvantages of morbidity rates—they are easily measured (and regularly so, for demographic purposes) and they are directly comparable between areas. Their use, however, as indicators of need can be challenged on the grounds that—

—'dead' people have no health need

—the main diseases which cause death (ischaemic heart disease, cancer and stroke) are neither the causes of most consultations nor is there much evidence that treatment can radically alter prognosis.

However, despite these disadvantages it can be argued that a population with a high mortality rate will also have a higher rate of other non-fatal diseases for which health services can help. In this way mortality rates can act as proxy-measures for morbidity. The extent to which this argument is correct supports the use of mortality rates as indicators of need.

iii. *Sickness absence.* Sickness absence rates or similar records of population illness can be used to judge whether one population compared with another has more illness. Here again, as in measuring patient-defined need through surveys of subjective impressions, factors other than health need contaminate the results. Factors such as tolerance to illness, job satisfaction and type of work may influence absence from work as much as health need. Moreover statistics such as sickness absence rates ignore large areas of morbidity such as among the unemployed, housewives, children and the retired.

iv. *Patient use of services.* Consultation rates or caseload is relatively easily obtained and as a measure of need recognized by the medical profession, might seem a good overall indicator. In using it, however, to compare areas it suffers from the disadvantage of reflecting two quite separate variables, namely, health need and the availability of services.

Compare two areas of equal population size:

> Area X: 20 000 consultations per annum
> Area Y: 40 000 consultations per annum

What do these figures mean? Do they mean that area Y has twice the need of area X because it has twice as many patients who consult? Or does it mean that area X has twice the need of area Y because it has half as many doctors who are available to see patients?

As was seen in the section on providing health care, 'unrestrained' demand for services probably outstrips supply. Therefore, if extra services are provided in one area—a new hospital, more doctors, etc., then the caseload will rise as the threshold is lowered, until the services are being fully used. (*See* Section 10.1 for further discussion.) Thus patients' use of health services reflects both their health need and the availability of those services, and in as much as these two determinants of use are almost impossible to separate then caseload figures are not very useful criteria for allocating health resources.

Conclusion

In any health care system it will be possible to identify a variety of different ways in which need is defined. This will partly reflect the influence of the different groups involved in health care, doctors, patients and government, which has evolved over the years and partly on any conscious effort to achieve some rational planning in the allocation of health resources.

9.3. Paying the doctor

Providing a 'free' health service at the point of use whether by an insurance mechanism or by direct payments from the State involves deciding what constitutes health need. It also involves the question of how best to pay the doctors, which in its turn can influence the definition of health need.

There are basically three methods of reimbursing the doctor and their relative advantages and disadvantages will be described, together with the influence they have on how health need comes to be defined.

a. Fee-for-service

This is the usual method of payment under the market system of providing health care. Here the doctor is paid a separate sum for each 'item' of service he provides. It is often found that this method of payment is also employed when insurance companies or governments intervene to cover patients for the costs of their care, the doctor charging them directly or indirectly for the services provided for insured patients.

The virtues of this system seem obvious. Doctors are paid, like many other skilled people, for the particular service rendered. If they work hard they receive a commensurate increase in income, if they choose to work only two days a week then they receive accordingly less. In short, fee-for-service acts as an incentive for the doctors to work hard.

In a manufacturing industry this system may have much to commend it—the harder the labour force works the greater the output and the larger the workers' incomes. Yet in providing health care to individual patients, the doctor's keenness to work might actually be counter-productive. Many medical problems may require the doctor to wait or be vigilant rather than be committed to speedy or heroic intervention.

Thus while fee-for-service may be suitable for other occupations it does raise problems in medicine: given the doctor's claim to be able to identify health needs it is the doctor who judges which service is necessary (not the consumer as in other situations) and thereby decides whether to collect a fee or not. In short, the doctor comes to have a vested interest in illness rather than in health. Slight menorrhagia, for example, may be more likely to become justification for an operation if the gynaecologist will be paid extra money than if he will not.

Although there are professional and ethical pressures to prevent financial criteria from affecting medical decision-making it has still proved necessary to organize widespread checks on medical practice when fee-for-service is the norm. In the United States, for example, peer review bodies will often assess the appropriateness of all surgery in a hospital and bring pressure to bear on those who seem to be 'over-operating'. As a peer group, it suffers from the potential bias that evaluation by fellow surgeons might introduce. It is now well established that those health services or parts of health services which have fee-for-service carry out more medical procedures, examinations, investigations, operations, etc., than those which do not.

Another example is afforded by the dental service within the NHS which mainly operates on a fee-for-service basis. Here checks are carried out by the Dental Estimates Board which approves fees for certain procedures and by checks on the quality of work performed. This of course can never exclude the possibility of unnecessary work. It has for example been suggested that a proportion of tooth cavities caused by caries would remineralize without treatment. However, in a fee-for-service system the incentive is for the dentist to drill out and fill the cavity rather than to wait. Indeed it is impossible to check on a wholly unscrupulous dentist who 'fills' a non-existent cavity and claims payment for doing so.

The other main problem with fee-for-service is that it can distort the definition of health need and health care in that it tends to reduce health to procedures which can be itemized for payment. For certain parts of medical practice this may be convenient but for many patient's problems, for which health must be widely defined (*see* Section 7.2), it tends to be inappropriate. Empathy, understanding and long-term emotional support, for example, are both difficult to itemize and indeed were they to be so, their nature might well be changed: 'friendship-for-a-fee' is very different from friendship.

b. Capitation

Capitation is a system by which the doctor is paid according to how many patients he looks after irrespective of whether they use his services. Thus two doctors with the same number of patients on their lists—and hence the same income—might work significantly different hours if one group of patients uses the service more than the other.

This system, in effect, works like the old Chinese method of paying the doctor whereby the doctor was paid by patients when they were healthy and not paid when they were ill. The doctor therefore receives a higher income, relative to the work performed, the healthier the population. The key advantage of this system is that the doctor (as well as the patient) profits from good health whereas under fee-for-service the doctor benefits from ill-health. Emphasis is therefore, in principle, placed on preventive measures, on support services and long-term care, etc., in an effort to improve the general health of the population served. (In contrast prevention under a fee-for-service system is in a somewhat ambivalent position because though it might gain an immediate fee it potentially reduces future earnings.)

One of the main problems with a system which works by encouraging current effort to improve patients' health is that it might not decrease future work-load. There is not sufficient evidence to support the belief that hard work by the doctor today will improve patients' health such that they consult less frequently in the future. Indeed it has even been argued that the opposite effect holds: over-concern with patients and their problems merely makes them more dependent and even more likely to consult in future. (*See* Section 10.1.)

The other problem with capitation is that instead of being concerned with their patients' health over time the doctor may come to be more concerned with how often they use the services offered. In other words, low consultation rates instead of being used as indicators of good health become ends in themselves. The result is that if the doctor wishes to increase income relative to work in-put there is an incentive to undertake the health care of too many patients and to give them only summary attention when they seek help.

c. Salary

The salary is, as it suggests, a fixed income irrespective of the work performed. It has the same advantages as capitation in that it acts as a disincentive to over-zealous and unnecessary investigation and treatment. Moreover it has an advantage over the capitation system in that there is no incentive to take on more patients than can reasonably be managed (though 'excess' patients might then find themselves on waiting lists and in queues—*see* Section 9.1). However it also has the same disadvantage in that there is no incentive to work hard. Even if there are fixed hours the doctor has no financial encouragement to work quickly and efficiently within them.

Conclusion

When comparing systems of paying the doctor it is as well to remember that, despite its undoubted appeal, money is not the only incentive behind good clinical practice. In the same way that the excesses of a fee-for-service system might be tempered by professional commitment to good medicine so the disincentives in the capitation and salaried systems are often overcome by doctors' pride and satisfaction in providing good medical care. The method of payment therefore, rather than dictating practice, tends to distort its emphasis, in particular how health need is defined and met by medical practitioners.

In any health care systems it is not unusual to find a mixture of methods of payment which illustrate the deficiencies of one or the other. Thus public health doctors are usually salaried even in an otherwise fee-for-service system and doctors paid by salary or capitation are often offered fees for specific services when these are deemed important enough to need encouraging, e.g. immunization, contraception.

Otherwise the chief disadvantages with salary and capitation as methods of payment have to be contrasted with those of fee-for-service. To a certain extent it might be argued that the tendency of capitation and salaried personnel to under-treat may be a more acceptable error than over-treatment, especially in view of the problems of effectiveness and efficiency of modern medicine. (*See* Chapter 10.) The other significant advantage of salary and capitation over fee-for-service is the relative cheapness of the former (at the expense of the medical profession who tend to gain from the latter). This acts as an incentive for governments to adopt the cheaper system; and its greater ability to encompass a wider definition of health, e.g. to include psycho-social factors, probably make it potentially more able to meet total health needs.

9.4. Managing the health service

The days are long past when the doctor could see himself as a solo practitioner, treating his patients in isolation from other doctors and health care professionals. The complexity of a modern health care system involves considerable 'administration' to co-ordinate its various components and as doctors and other health professionals play such a central role in the actual provision of health care, they are inevitably drawn into the administrative structure either in an official capacity or simply to plead their own particular case.

A detailed consideration of administrative and management theories cannot be provided here. Instead an outline is offered of some of the key concepts behind the great variety of different theories the student may encounter in further reading.

One of the interminable debates about managing a health service is concerned with the question, 'What is the best management structure?' Structure here refers to the formal and informal relationships people have as members of organizations. Two possible structures, for example, of a health care team might be:

—a pyramidal structure in which decisions are taken, say, by the doctor to whom the other personnel are responsible. Thus:

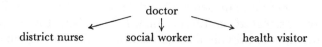

—an 'arena' structure in which decisions are taken jointly and accountability is to the team.

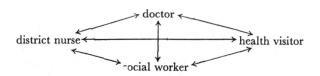

To answer the question Which of these is better? we must know something of the criteria by which they are to be compared. Three concepts, goals, technology and ideology, have an important influence on the criteria we select.

i. *Goals*. Deciding on the best management structure involves consideration of what the organization is trying to do. These latter constitute the organization's goals. If the goal of a factory is to produce cars then, other things being equal, the factory which produces the most cars can claim the better administrative structure. On the other hand the goal might be seen as profits or a satisfied work-force, in which case the management structure would reflect these various aims. In the former the factory might be run by means of a hierarchical structure which entailed close supervision and monitoring of all employees, in the latter it might be run with greater worker participation in management.

ii. *Technology*. The technology employed by an organization is the technical means used to achieve the organization's goals. A car production line in which every worker performs a small repetitive task requires a different management structure than a factory in which the complete car is built totally by a small group of workers at their own pace. In the same way changes in technology in the health service such as disposable syringes, new drugs, dialysis machines, electric floor polishers, improvements in psychotherapy, etc., may result in changes in the management structure to match the changes in the work itself.

iii. *Ideology*. Whereas technology refers to the technical means of achieving goals, ideology refers to the social and psychological beliefs about acceptable means. In the two classic management theories 'scientific management' and 'human relations' different emphases are placed on interpersonal factors. Scientific management attempts to provide a set of clear-cut rules for organizing a group of workers: everyone should have a particular, clearly defined job, everyone should know to whom they are accountable and who is accountable to them and decisions are made according to the fixed rules of the organization.

The human relations school, on the other hand, claims that people work more efficiently if there is some flexibility in their work rules. This theory stresses the importance of interpersonal contact, some degree of worker autonomy to decide how best to do a job and an interest in the workers as people, in contrast to the very mechanistic view of scientific management.

The reason why alternative theories such as these can both flourish without one being shown to be 'better' is because beliefs on how an organization should be structured become particularly important when goals are unclear. Comparing the means towards an end can then become as important as comparing ends themselves. In most large organizations a multiplicity of goals can be identified—often mutually conflicting—and in that various management structures meet some but not all of these goals it is difficult to label one structure as better than another overall.

How do these concepts apply to the administration of a health service? The problem can be illustrated at different levels of organization.

a. Managing the health service

The goal of a health service is ostensibly to meet health need but, as has been discussed earlier, there is no objective means of defining that particular goal. Instead there tends to be a variety of competing definitions from doctors, patients, nurses, administrators, etc. The doctor may be interested in cure rate, the administrator in hospital discharges, the patient in patient well-being, the laboratory technician in work load and so on. Without any consensus on goals there can be no agreement on appropriate management structure.

This problem is exacerbated by the special position of the health professionals, especially the doctor, in the health service. Whatever the formal administrative structure—the chain of authority, the lines of accountability, etc.—the doctors remain outside because of their clinical autonomy. This separation from the formal management structure is justified on the grounds that the nature of medical work demands that it is free from external control. The result is that in a health service a curious mixture of organizations usually prevails: a traditional authority structure or bureaucracy in which all are accountable and the medical profession who are only accountable to their patients (though this is somewhat nominal in view of their patients' inability to fully evaluate clinical decisions).

This dual system can lead to problems because of the inability of management to influence clinicians and the non-accountability of clinicians when they consume, on the patient's behalf, resources which are nominally controlled by management. The result can be serious disagreement and antagonism between clinicians and administrators and consequent failure to allocate resources, finance, equipment, staff, etc., to their best advantage.

b. Managing the hospital

The use of goals, technology and ideology in analysing hospital administration can be illustrated by an example.

Until the early 1950s most schizophrenics had been treated by long-term hospitalization. Mental hospitals had merely exerted a custodial function over their inmates and the organizational structure reflected the particular goal of segregating these patients from the 'normal' community outside. By the early 1960s the mental hospitals had been transformed, fewer patients were hospitalized and those that were stayed for shorter periods. The management structure inside the hospitals reflected this optimism about the prognosis of schizophrenia: it became less hierarchical, less rule-bound, more informal. What had happened in the intervening years?

i. *Technological change.* The phenothiazine drugs had been introduced in the mid-1950s and this might explain the sudden change in goals. From aiming towards long-term custody the hospitals could now try for early discharge following the improvements in prognosis brought about by the new drugs.

ii. *Ideological change.* The counter to the above argument is that the change in mental hospital policy occurred because of a change in ideas about how schizophrenia or madness should be viewed. Instead of being seen as a dangerous, potentially violent illness which required separating from the community it became viewed like any other incapacitating illness which required tolerance and understanding. Supporters of this line of argument can point to several hospitals which started the new regime of early discharge before the new drugs were available and they can point to a great interest in the nature of mental illness during these years which manifested itself, for example, in a Royal Commission on mental health in Britain.

The point, though, is not to establish here which is the better explanation but rather to see the often quite complex ramifications of these different factors. Whether mental hospitals should be run like general hospitals or as therapeutic communities or indeed whether there should be separate mental hospitals at all can only be answered in the context of the technological means available of achieving certain goals, the ideological beliefs about mental illness and the goals themselves in a particular mental health service.

c. *Managing the ward*

Whenever the reports of ill-treatment of patients in hospitals arise they almost always seem to centre on long stay, chronic illness, geriatric or psychiatric wards. Why should these be at the centre of many problems when surgical wards for example hardly feature?

Surgical wards are relatively easy to organize. The goals, and means by which they should be achieved, can readily be identified for each member of staff from surgeon to nurse to cleaner. There is complex technology available in achieving that goal and surgery itself represents a highly prestigious aspect of medical practice.

In contrast, the long-term ward has a problem in identifying goals which all staff can work towards. There are no 'cures' and few discharges by which to measure success. The surgical ward nurse can see at the end of the week what has been accomplished, whereas on the long-stay ward the week passes like any other, unmarked by feedback on what has been achieved or what has been improved upon.

The goal, if there is one, is 'care' but how is this to be identified? There is little high technology, only human relationships, and these are meant to be directed at a goal which is difficult to assess. How can good care be maintained or increased if it cannot be measured?

Because of this uncertain feature of work on long-stay wards it has been suggested that goal displacement tends to occur whereby staff choose goals other than care by which to measure the accomplishments and progress in their daily routine. These new goals often tend to relate to simple administrative criteria such as the regular delivery of soap and towels to the ward or in the efficient disposal of dirty linen or the regularity of meals and general neatness of the ward. Staff can take pride in these achievements which are visible to them and to outsiders.

Gradually however these new administrative goals can take precedence over the caring goals for which the ward was established. In extreme cases they totally displace them to the neglect of the patient or even to the point where consideration of patients' welfare becomes an impediment to achieving the new goals. Thus the informal goals of staff members can function to undermine the formal caring goals of a hospital ward.

Organizations in perspective

Contradictory advice on how to manage the various levels of a health service abound. These conflicts do not reflect our ignorance of the best way but rather on the various assumptions of technological input, ideological beliefs and particular goals. These differences can rarely be reconciled by testing and comparing how health service facilities *do* work in practice; rather they represent our often implicit assumptions of what we think a health service *should* be doing and how it should be doing it.

9.5. Informal health care

So far in this chapter some of the various problems of organizing and delivering a formal health care system have been discussed. However, this has meant that the major part of the health care provided in a society has been ignored; most health care is in fact 'organized' and 'delivered' within the home, mainly within families, on an 'informal' basis.

a. Health care in the home

Although the exact extent of informal health care is unknown various forms of morbidity which are managed within the home can be identified.

i. Virtually all the illnesses which go unreported to doctors. (*See* Section 3.1.)

ii. Almost all patients under a doctor who are not hospitalized are, at least in part, cared for within the home.

iii. Most chronic illness, much of it serious and incapacitating.

iv. Many patients discharged home from hospital for convalescence or continuing care.

v. Many people who are dying receive terminal care within the home.

The formal health care system thus only constitutes the tip of the iceberg, a small, if expensive part of the total health care provided in a society: care in the home is the hidden part of the iceberg.

In the main the role of the formal health care system is to care for people whose illnesses are too difficult and too serious to be managed solely within the home but this demarcation is dependent on the adequacy of resources in both formal and informal care sectors. On the one hand resources within the health care system are rarely adequate to completely cover all who need such care so that many people with serious and debilitating conditions must 'cope' at home, perhaps with the help of a close relative. On the other hand, resources such as facilities, skills and support may be lacking in the home and the patient must be either accepted into hospital (often as a so-called 'social admission') or found a place within another institution, such as an old people's home or nursing home, which can in effect provide the resources and care that the patient's own home lacks.

b. Community care

It is increasingly felt that the care given within the home and family in the community should be seen as an integral part of the health care system. Moreover it appears that care in the home is not simply an amateur version of hospital care, but may, in many ways, be superior. Thus the policy of many countries is to encourage home care and support it with more resources from the formal health care system on a community basis: hence an emphasis on 'community care'.

General practitioners can manage more health problems in the community without the patient being hospitalized. The community or district nurse can treat problems in the patient's own home which would otherwise have required hospital nursing care. Provision of home helps to look after domestic chores or meals-on-wheels to provide food can supplement home resources. Grants and benefits to those willing to stay at home and look after aged incapacitated relatives can prevent such people from being permanently institutionalized. And so on.

These attempts to bolster the power of informal care to look after more people in the community might be welcomed on the basis that home care is generally preferable to the anonymity of hospital care. However two criticisms of community care have been made which deserve consideration.

i. *A cost saving device.* To a certain extent formal and informal health care systems are complementary such that if one system defaults the other tends to compensate. This apparent reciprocity between the systems, it has been argued, has been seized on by governments intent on reducing expenditure on formal health care services. Thus it is possible to dispense with expensive hospital-based services by giving a vague and perhaps token commitment to community care. But what in fact happens is that the increased resources going to community care are wholly inadequate and it is left to the informal care system to pick up the pieces.

The net effect is a commendable saving and reduction in government spending but a comparable (and hidden) additional cost falling on families with illness. Costs are therefore removed from the whole community (in terms of government expenditure) and placed on individual families with the illnesses who may well be the least able to bear the increased demands.

Commitment to community care must therefore be seen in the context of where costs for this service tend to fall. Community care when adequately provided is a very different phenomenon from when it over-relies on the informal care system—which might well be weighed down with its own problems anyway.

ii. *Problems of family care.* Care of the ill in their own home might be a worth while ideal but it often rather depends on ill people living in an 'ideal' home.

Many ill people, especially the elderly, who might benefit from care by their immediate families are unable to obtain it because they don't live in a 'family unit'. Old people living alone and single parents often find that there is no-one who might be in a position to offer care.

Having an ill person in the home can lead to extra expense: heating, lighting, cleaning, food, shopping, special facilities, etc. These additional costs which would otherwise be carried by insurance or hospitals are placed on families which look after their ill at home.

The largest additional cost, however, is more difficult to quantify and relates to the problems involved in finding someone within the family to actually do the caring. One of the traditional tasks for women, besides running the home, was to look after members of the family who fell ill (women themselves not being expected to become ill). However, with the changing role of women in contemporary society, more having full-time jobs, perhaps more sharing of domestic tasks, it can be difficult to find someone to actually do the caring. Who should take time off work? Who should get up at night? What costs in terms of added tensions and friction within the home are incurred?

One of the main problems is that we know so little about care in the home, its costs and its benefits. In many situations it might well be the best treatment; in others it might be inappropriate for either the well-being of the patient or domestic harmony. Medical trials of 'home' versus 'hospital' treatment for various problems rarely attempt to evaluate these costs on the family. Despite our ignorance of the extent and limits of informal care it would be wrong to take it for granted.

Further reading

Abel-Smith B. 1976
Value for Money in Health Services. London, Heinemann.
   Further discussion of many of the issues raised in this chapter.
Mahler H. 1975
Health: a demystification of medical technology. *Lancet* **2,** 829–833.
   Argues that Western medicine often pursues high technology as a goal in its own right.
George V. and Wilding P. 1976
Ideology and Social Welfare. London, Routledge & Kegan Paul.
   Political views are important in the provision of health care and this book summarizes the various political attitudes to a State-provided health service.

10 *Evaluating health care*

This final section discusses some of the problems associated with evaluating health care. It should help to summarize and consolidate many of the ideas covered in earlier chapters. The approach will be first of all to develop a model which clarifies the different points in the health care systems which are open to evaluation and secondly to discuss some of these issues in closer detail.

Health care systems can be analysed in terms of three variables:

  i. A person has a *need* for health care.

  ii. They *use* the health service to meet that need.

  iii. Intervention of the health service resources produces a certain *outcome*.

  iv. The outcome may in its turn constitute a further need for health services, e.g. an amputation creates a further need for rehabilitation services, thus —

10.1. Use of health services

The concept of health need has been discussed in Section 9.2 There it was argued that there is no 'real' need which can be objectively established, rather need is a concept which varies according to the party defining it. However, whatever way health need is defined need must be translated into *demand* if the health services are to be used (except for certain medical screening programmes that might be brought to the patient).

Thus:

$$\text{need} \longrightarrow (\text{demand}) \longrightarrow \text{use}.$$

Secondly, given the existence of a patient demand, the health services can only be used if they are *available*. Demand for an ophthalmic service, for example, which is not provided locally cannot manifest itself in use.

Thus:

$$\text{need} \longrightarrow \text{(demand)} \longrightarrow \text{(availability)} \longrightarrow \text{use.}$$

As was pointed out in Section 9.2. the caseload (use) figures for two regions of a health service cannot be used as indicators of health need as they also represent aspects of illness behaviour (*see* Chapter 2 for how patient needs become translated into demand for health services) and the availability of the services demanded. In summary, data on use of health services reflect three separate factors: (i) health need, (ii) illness behaviour, (iii) availability of services.

In practice it has proved very difficult to separate these components of any utilization data. However, this has not prevented two important hypotheses concerning the use of health services to be advanced.

a. The Inverse Care Law

The Inverse Care Law was suggested by Tudor Hart in 1971 to explain what he believed was a fundamental inequality in the provision of health services. The 'Law' is simply that those with the greatest need have the poorest services. In essence he was examining the relationship:

$$\text{need} \longrightarrow \text{(availability)} \longrightarrow \text{use}$$

and suggesting that whereas the availability of services should in some way reflect need:

$$\text{need} \propto \text{(availability)} \longrightarrow \text{use}$$

they in fact reflected the polar opposite:

$$\text{need} \propto \frac{1}{\text{availability}} \longrightarrow \frac{1}{\text{use.}}$$

Need was inversely related to availability and hence to use. In short those with greatest health need had the poorest services and those with least need had the best.

The argument as originally advanced used social class differences as its basis though it has since enjoyed wider currency and is often applied to other seemingly disadvantaged groups such as the old and the chronically ill. The original argument can be broken down into three claims: (i) Working class people have a greater need than the middle class. (ii) The working class has fewer health resources available to them, i.e. need $\propto$ 1/availability. (iii) The working class consequently under-uses the health services relative to their need, i.e. need $\propto$ 1/use.

i. Evidence for the first statement arises from measuring various dimensions of need. (*See* Section 9.2.) Although each of these variables is arguably deficient in some respect, together they present a fairly convincing picture of greater health need in the working class population. Major differences in mortality rates and morbidity rates (using various measures) are consistently found between the social classes.

ii. Finding evidence to support the second statement is more difficult. In his original argument Tudor Hart used the fact that GP surgeries in working class districts tended to be older than those in middle-class districts—which though it might be significant is not clear evidence of a difference in the quality of care given—and the fact that as most doctors were recruited from middle-class families (some 80% from social classes I and II) they would offer a poorer service to working class people for whom they would have little understanding. Again, this second charge is not conclusive although it has some circumstantial evidence to support it in that one study found GPs giving longer consultations to middle class patients and covering more problems. Whether GPs from working class backgrounds would respond any differently, however, is open to question.

More evidence for resource inequalities between social classes comes indirectly from geographical comparisons. It has been found, for example, that the south-east of England which has a disproportionate number of middle class people has relatively more resources than the rest of the country, especially compared with those areas with high working class populations. Yet even here the actual distribution of health care within the regions remains unknown. The conclusion must be that definitive evidence is lacking, though there is circumstantial support for inequalities of health care resource by social class.

iii. There are more statistics available for evaluation of the third statement. As was pointed out in Chapter 2 it is now well recognized that the working class under-utilize preventive services such as screening, dental care, postnatal examinations, immunization, etc. For primary health care there are also class differences in consultation rates though these seem to favour the working class (*Table* 15).

Table 15. GP CONSULTATIONS PER YEAR BY SOCIAL CLASS

		Average number consultations per annum
Social class	I	2·6
	II	2·8
	IIIn	3·2
	IIIm	3·4
	IV	3·2
	V	4·3

However, these figures need to be interpreted in the light of the two other determinants of use: health need and illness behaviour. It might be argued that—

—the figures take no account of relative need

—many of the working class consultations are for sickness certificates which they tend to require more often for work than middle class people.

The effect of these two factors is difficult to establish but relating consultation patterns to measures of morbidity would suggest rough equivalence in consulting rates and allowing for 'certificate consultations' would support the existence of the Inverse Care Law in general practice.

The problem, however, with evidence which supports the existence of under-utilization relative to health need is that it is not necessarily due to non-availability of facilities (i.e. assumption (ii) is not necessary for (i) and (iii) to be correct). The argument of the Inverse Care Law is that under-utilization, given a certain level of need, is a reflection of the availability of health care resources whereas, as was argued earlier, it could just as much be a product of different patterns of illness behaviour in working class groups affecting the actual demand for those services.

i.e.

$$\text{need} \xrightarrow{\substack{\text{illness} \\ \text{behaviour}}} \text{(demand)} \longrightarrow \text{(availability)} \longrightarrow \text{use.}$$

Even if, say, preventive services are offered and made available to a working-class population they may not use them because of their particular culture concerning the value of planning ahead for good health.

The argument which can be used against this 'cultural' explanation, however, is that the offer and availability of these under-used services is in such a middle class form that there is no congruence with working class values. Thus availability in the form of opening the clinic doors and saying 'come and use it when you need to' reflects more middle class values towards health than working class. It may be necessary to try other means to influence working class behaviour. An anti-smoking campaign which stresses that smoking produces lung cancer after many years may appeal more to a middle class audience whereas a campaign which suggests smoking is becoming socially unacceptable or that it is a sign of weakness may have greater success in another culture.

Notwithstanding the difficulties in deciding the applicability of the Inverse Care Law to social class and health, the evidence for other areas is more clear. This section has concentrated on social class partly because it was the basis of the original Law and partly because it illustrates many of the problems of evaluating and analysing health care statistics. Yet as far as the so-called 'Cinderella' areas of medicine are concerned particularly mental and physical handicap, geriatrics and parts of psychiatry, the relative lack of very basic amenities such as reasonable food and living conditions constitutes evidence of a distortion of priorities in the provision of care.

b. Iatrogenesis

The other important argument about the use of health services is the iatrogenic hypothesis suggested by Illich. His argument divides into two parts.

Firstly, he argues that clinical iatrogenesis (i.e. doctor-induced disease) is increasing. Thus in using the health service for a relatively minor health problem the patient runs the risk of being subjected to investigations and treatments which produce a worse health problem than the original one.

This argument is not new and clinicians have been aware of it for many years. Knowledge is accumulating of the dangers of many drug combinations and of the side effects of treatments and investigations and it seems reasonable to hope that such forms of iatrogenic disease are minimized.

Increase in iatrogenic disease may paradoxically represent therapeutic advances which enable some patients to either live longer or more satisfying lives despite having a serious disease. In the end, however, they succumb to the drug therapy rather than the disease which it is holding at bay and become a case of iatrogenic disease. Thus steroid therapy in young people may hold off debilitating illnesses though in later life the Cushing syndrome which is induced will itself cause problems of medical management.

The second and much more striking of Illich's arguments concerns the 'social and structural' iatrogenic effects of medicine. Illich argues that the general availability of health care to the population has resulted in increasing dependence on doctors. Whereas in the past people had to cope with their own problems and minor symptoms today they can go to the doctor to talk, to get advice, to obtain drugs, etc.

Illich's ideas are discussed more fully in Section 8.5 but it is worth reiterating the contrast with the Inverse Care Law. In the latter the claim is that non-availability of health services is detrimental to the health of sections of the population whereas for Illich it is the converse: that too great an availability of health services is damaging people's health. Liberal health service provision actually encourages people to use the health service more than they 'really' need. Over time they gradually become dependent on this over-use feeling it is a necessary part of being healthy. But, claims Illich, this dependence is itself a form of sickness which undermines the good health of autonomous human beings.

In essence Illich is arguing that the availability of services not only links health need with use but also actually generates the health need it purports to be meeting. Thus:

$$\overset{\frown}{\text{need}} \longrightarrow \quad \text{(availability)} \longrightarrow \quad \text{use.}$$

He therefore argues that providing more health services to meet apparent need is both counter-productive and harmful. Increasing health services creates more need (by reducing people's thresholds), greater use and in consequence demand for even more services, which in turn is met by increasing resources and so on. In effect a vicious circle of need, of demand and resources is created.

Some support for this model can be found in the apparent exponential growth in health services in the Western world over the last few decades while self-assessment of health or sickness absence rates seem to deteriorate. It has also been argued that simply making services available does encourage increased use. Thus, for example, the different rates of surgical operations found in the US and the UK seem to bear a closer relationship to the relative numbers of surgeons in these two countries than to any more direct indicators of need for surgery. It has also been found that when GPs attempt to reduce the pressure on their surgeries by taking on another partner or extending the length of their clinics the consultation rate in the practice tends to rise and consultations tend to take longer. In short, increased resources allocated to health care often only seem to uncover further demand.

The fact that demand seems to rise in line with resources could equally well be explained by claiming real unmet need is being uncovered rather than that dependency is being created. In short, particular 'evidence' is unlikely to confirm or refute the validity of Illich's argument for the latter rests on the assumption that a healthy person is an autonomous person: dependence on other people for advice, for help, for treatment, etc., reduces autonomy and thereby destroys health. These contrasting views of Illich and Hart can only be reconciled if it is realized that they have very different political and social values which reflect in the way they see health. For one, some degree of dependence on medical services is quite congruent with good health while for the other, dependency itself is a form of illness.

10.2. Outcome

A health problem has its own natural history. At some point in time we can see where the natural history of the problem has reached and call this the outcome.

Thus:

$$\text{health problems} \xrightarrow{\text{natural history}} \text{outcome N.}$$

The goal of a health service is to intervene in the natural history of the problem using certain resources or inputs to produce a more desirable outcome.

Thus:

health problems   ⎯⎯⎯⎯⟶   outcome D.

↗

input

However, health problems do not bear a one-to-one relationship to input of resources. Two patients, one with lung cancer, the other with pneumonia, might consume vastly different quantities of health resources. Yet consumption of many resources, surgical, nursing, radiotherapeutic, pharmacological, etc., by the cancer patient may fail to change the prognosis, while the prescription of relatively cheap antibiotics may radically alter the chances for the patient with pneumonia. In other words, resource input must be seen in the context of its effectiveness.

Thus:

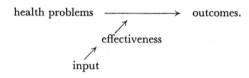

a. Comparing health services

In comparing two different health care systems, or one system over time, it is necessary to use some measure of outcome: if a system has a better outcome at some point in time that system might be described as 'better'. One common outcome measure of a health care system is infant mortality rate (mortality in the first year of life).

Consider the rates in *Table* 16. These figures show Sweden as having the lowest rate so does this make Swedish health care better than the other two? There are various factors to consider.

Table 16.   INFANT MORTALITY RATES BY SELECTED COUNTRIES

	Infant mortality rate
Sweden	10·8
England & Wales	17·2
Italy	27·0

First, it is not possible to argue that the Swedish system is better than England's or Italy's because the health needs which are to be met by the system may vary considerably. As was pointed out in earlier sections health need is dependent on many non-medical factors such as nutrition, sanitation, etc. Thus if for some reason there are four times as many premature births in Italy than Sweden then the poor output measure of the Italian system may still reflect a high quality health care system.

Secondly, use of services may affect the outcome figures. Even if the health need in Sweden and Italy was exactly the same, the higher Italian mortality rate might be a reflection of the population's failure to use existing services. Socio-cultural factors in the population can therefore be seen to have some effect on both the level of need and use of the health service and consequently on any outcome measures irrespective of the quality of care provided.

In summary, outcome measures of a health service are the product of four different factors:

   i. *Health need* as manifested in the natural history of health problems.

   ii. *Use* as affected by illness behaviour patterns.

   iii. The level of resource *input*.

   iv. The *effectiveness* of the health care input, i.e.

$$\text{health problem (need)} \longrightarrow \underset{\nearrow}{\text{use}} \longrightarrow \text{outcome.}$$
$$\text{effectiveness}$$
$$\nearrow$$
$$\text{input}$$

Because of the difficulties inherent in measuring and using outcome, many international comparisons are based on health service inputs. Input measures frequently found are GNP per capita spent on health and numbers of doctors per 100 000 population.

Yet again these figures can be misleading (*Table* 17). A comparison of Swedish, English and Italian health services by this input statistic offers the complete opposite to that of infant

Table 17. NUMBER OF DOCTORS PER 100 000 POPULATION BY SELECTED COUNTRIES

	No. of doctors per 100 000 population
Sweden	100
England & Wales	104
Italy	164

mortality. Whereas using infant mortality Sweden, with the lowest figure, would seem to provide the best health service, on number of doctors, Italy with the most, could claim to have the best.

The assumption behind input comparisons is that 'more is better' and this is not necessarily true for most health services. This is because—

—The distribution of health care resources in many countries is uneven, often with concentrations in urban areas, which means that rural health consequently suffers.

—The same quantity of resources may vary in quality, i.e. effectiveness.

b. Outcomes of health services

In discussing comparisons of health services it has been assumed that we know what the outcomes are, though they might prove difficult to measure. There is, however, a considerable difference between what we imagine or expect a health service to achieve and what it actually does. It would probably be fair to say that the rationale for providing a health service is that it will have therapeutic benefit on the health of the population. Yet what it actually achieves is probably much wider. We might isolate two important effects: (i) therapeutic, (ii) social.

i. *Therapeutic effects.* While these might be the chief rationale for a health service it is clear from the discussion on measurement that these are difficult to quantify as many factors other than the existence of a health service seem to affect therapeutic outcomes. Indeed, using the arguments advanced in Chapter 7 on the influence of social factors on morbidity and mortality, it might be argued that the specific therapeutic effect of a health service is probably fairly low in terms of lives saved or people cured— housing or diet for example probably have greater influence. Yet to evaluate medicine by mortality would be needlessly to restrict it to a narrow range of operation. McKeown has argued that the role of medicine is wider than this: 'To assist us to come safely into the world and comfortably out of it, and during life to protect the well and care for the sick and disabled.' Though these goals may be less glamorous than those of curative medicine they may be no less socially desirable and while they too present considerable measurement problems (What is good care?) it is apparent that in the context of the huge demands made on health services for health care they probably represent the most important outcome criteria of therapeutic effectiveness.

ii. *Social effects*. As was pointed out in Chapter 6 health services have social as well as therapeutic functions and the 'social role of medicine' in terms of the social control function it exerts must be seen as one of the major effects of the health service irrespective of its therapeutic efficacy.

c. Outcome of treatment

It has been recognized for many years that the evaluation of specific treatment regimens has been susceptible to the *post hoc ergo propter hoc* fallacy, that is the particular outcome of a treatment has been interpreted as being brought about by the treatment, whereas it in fact was the natural outcome of the disease process. Thus any treatment might seem effective in a self-limiting disease.

The way round this problem was discovered several decades ago when the random controlled clinical trial came into use. In these, patients for whom a certain treatment might be of benefit are randomly allocated to an experimental and a control group. The experimental group receives the treatment (preferably 'blind'), the control group a placebo and the outcome of the two groups is compared.

Thus:

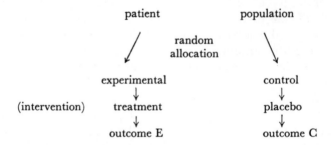

If outcome E is better than outcome C then the treatment is effective and if outcomes are similar then the treatment is ineffective. It has been argued that with these techniques the use of various treatment regimes in medicine can be objectively evaluated. While this claim is true in part there are certain difficulties which cannot be overcome even by better experimental design.

i. *Selection of outcome indicators.* When two drugs are being compared in a random control trial (RCT) it might be found that drug A is better than drug B because it saves more lives or that drug C is better than drug D because it relieves more pain. Both these outcome criteria are selections from a potentially long list, e.g. death, comfort, happiness, ability to work, normal blood film, etc., and they represent selections from different criteria over time, e.g. comfort → pain → death.

Thus, though drug A might save more lives than drug B over a 5-year period drug B might also enable more people to go back to work. Though drug C may relieve more pain than drug D, D may improve the long-term prognosis. Many of these variations in outcome are known: certain drugs reduce hypertension but produce impotence, certain drugs relieve epilepsy but damage the fetus, etc. Yet compared with the outcomes—good and bad—that are known, most outcomes are unknown either because they have not been thought important enough to measure or they are too difficult to measure. Coronary care units may be no more effective in terms of mortality than home care for myocardial infarction, but what of patient contentment, family relations, anxiety, social cost, etc.? If these criteria were used coronary care units might be more (or less) effective than care at home.

This is not to argue simply for an extension of outcome criteria to wider social variables, but to point to inherent constraints in evaluating two therapies. We can never know all the effects, but the effects we do choose to look at will in certain ways bias the service we provide. If we restrict outcome measures to mortality we may create a health service which emphasizes extended life at the expense of other, perhaps important, aspects of people's lives.

ii. *Individual versus community needs.* Even accepting that within certain constraints one treatment is better than another, does this justify its use on a patient who would benefit from it? The answer may seem obvious. Yet given that the resources of a health service are finite, then by providing one patient with an effective therapy for a problem another patient is deprived of those same resources. If renal dialysis is provided for a patient, the cost of that treatment is not then available to provide care for a geriatric patient, or an improved antenatal service, or radiotherapy for a cancer. In these terms the doctor's action in helping one patient is, paradoxically, depriving another patient. Thus though doctors are taught to treat individual patients to the best of their ability, and though they may be wise enough only to use effective methods, doctors are in fact constantly making non-individual judgements, as their decision to treat a patient is also a decision to allocate resources away from other potential patients the doctor probably has not even seen or may not know about. Every treatment is in effect a judgement on priorities within that society.

In the end individual health problems must be seen in the context of community needs, resources and priorities.

Further reading

Cochrane A. 1972
Effectiveness and Efficiency. London, Nuffield.
A book which urges on the medical profession the value of the randomized controlled trial.

Tudor Hart J. 1971
The Inverse Care Law. *Lancet* **i**, 405–412.

Index